THEotherAMERICA

ILLEGAL Immigrants

by
Gail B. Stewart

Photographs by
Natasha Frost

Lucent Books, P.O. Box 289011, San Diego, CA 92198-9011

These and other titles are included in *The Other America* series:

Battered Women

The Elderly

Gangs

Gay and Lesbian Youth

The Homeless

Illegal Immigrants

People with AIDS

Teen Mothers

Teen Runaways

Teens in Prison

Cover design: Carl Franzen

Library of Congress Cataloging-in-Publication Data

Stewart, Gail, 1949-
    Illegal immigrants / by Gail B. Stewart ; photographs by Natasha Frost.
      p. cm. — (The other America)
    Includes bibliographical references and index.
    Summary: Uses the first-person accounts of four illegal immigrants to discuss the situations and concerns related to the problematic issue.
    ISBN 1-56006-339-4 (alk. paper)
    1. Immigrants—Southwest, New—Social conditions—Juvenile literature.   2. Illegal aliens—Southwest, New—Social conditions—Juvenile literature.   3. Southwest, New—Emigration and immigration—Social aspects—Juvenile literature.   [1. Illegal aliens. 2. United States—Emigration and immigration.]   I. Frost, Natasha, ill. II. Series: Stewart, Gail, 1949– Other America.
    JV6565.S74   1997
    305.9'0693—dc20   96–33600
                                           CIP
                                           AC

The opinions of and stories told by the people in this book are entirely their own. The author has presented their accounts in their own words, and has not verified their accuracy. Thus, the author can make no claim as to the objectivity of their accounts.

Printed in the U.S.A.
Copyright © 1997 by Lucent Books, Inc.
P.O. Box 289011, San Diego, CA 92198-9011

B 30330

Contents

Foreword

O, YES,
I SAY IT PLAIN,
AMERICA NEVER WAS AMERICA TO ME.
AND YET I SWEAR THIS OATH—
AMERICA WILL BE!
LANGSTON HUGHES

Perhaps more than any other nation in the world, the United States represents an ideal to many people. The ideal of equality—of opportunity, of legal rights, of protection against discrimination and oppression. To a certain extent, this image has proven accurate. But beneath this ideal lies a less idealistic fact—many segments of our society do not feel included in this vision of America.

They are the outsiders—the homeless, the elderly, people with AIDS, teenage mothers, gang members, prisoners, and countless others. When politicians and the media discuss society's ills, the members of these groups are defined as what's wrong with America; they are the people who need fixing, who need help, or increasingly, who need to take more responsibility. And as these people become society's fix-it problem, they lose all identity as individuals and become part of an anonymous group. In the media and in our minds these groups are identified by condition—a disease, crime, morality, poverty. Their condition becomes their identity, and once this occurs, in the eyes of society, they lose their humanity.

The Other America series reveals the members of these groups as individuals. Through in-depth interviews, each person tells his or her unique story. At times these stories are painful, revealing individuals who are struggling to maintain their integrity, their humanity, their lives, in the face of fear, loss, and economic and spiritual hardship. At other times, their tales are exasperating, demonstrating a litany of poor choices, shortsighted thinking, and self-gratification. Nevertheless, their identities remain distinct, their personalities diverse.

As we listen to the people of *The Other America* series describe their experiences they cease to be stereotypically defined and become tangible, individual. In the process, we may begin to understand more profoundly and think more critically about society's problems. When politicians debate, for example, whether the homeless problem is due to a poor economy or lack of initiative, it will help to read the words of the homeless. Perhaps then we can see the issue more clearly. The family who finds itself temporarily homeless because it has always been one paycheck from poverty is not the same as the mother of six who has been chronically chemically dependent. These people's circumstances are not all of one kind, and perhaps we, after all, are not so very different from them. Before we can act to solve the problems of the Other America, we must be willing to look down their path, to see their faces. And perhaps in doing so, we may find a piece of ourselves as well.

Introduction

THE FACTS ABOUT ILLEGAL IMMIGRANTS

Twenty-two-year-old Juan remembers the night very clearly, although he was only six at the time: "I was holding on to my mother's hand," he says. "I was not supposed to talk. She had told me and my two sisters over and over that we weren't to say anything, even if someone asked us a question.

"We were half-running, half-walking across a field, part of a ranch, I think. We were trying to get to the road where there would be a truck waiting for us. We could hear shouting and men's voices. Was it the border patrol? Was it a group of men waiting in the dark to rob us? We didn't know.

"It seemed like hours that we were running, hurrying toward the road," he says. "I had to go to the bathroom, but I knew we couldn't stop. My legs hurt, and I was afraid. Then all of a sudden we were at the road, and there was a truck. A man was motioning us to hurry, hurry, *rapido*! We jumped into the back and sped away to another place, to another truck that would take us to a place where we would be safe."

THE DREAM OF A BETTER LIFE

"That was the longest night of our lives, I think—and it was all about coming to the United States. And even though we made it to the truck that night and to the city where we could find a place to stay, we still were afraid for a very long time afterwards. Every knock on the door, every time we saw a policeman, we wondered: Would this be the time we get found out? Would this be the time we'd be sent back across the border?"

Juan's story is hardly unusual; it happens thousands of times every day in the United States. People who are not citizens of this country secretly cross the borders, bringing little with them except the dream of a better life for themselves and their children. Often they are caught and sent back across the border, only to risk their lives trying again.

These people are known as illegal immigrants, those who wish to live in the United States but cannot or do not gain entry through proper channels. The United States currently accepts about seven hundred thousand new immigrants legally each year—more than all other countries in the world combined. Those who are granted entry are selected based on certain factors, such as being related to a U.S. citizen or having job skills that are valuable to the American economy.

The chances of those who are unskilled workers or without family or relatives in the United States are very slim. Some of those wait for entry permits, hoping they can be admitted under a category called nonpreference, but few are successful. Most of those who do not meet the restrictions imposed by the U.S. government enter illegally, either by crossing the border secretly, or by presenting fake documents to border officials.

While no one can be sure exactly how many illegal immigrants come to the United States each year, border patrols report that they apprehended more than one million illegal immigrants last year. The Immigration and Naturalization Service (INS) estimated that in 1995 there were between four and six million illegal immigrants in the United States, with the numbers increasing by three hundred thousand each year. The presence of these illegals in the United States, while not a major concern for some, is a threat to other Americans, who see the illegal immigrants as a financial and social problem.

"THE SECRET OF AMERICA"

The irony of it all is that America is a nation of immigrants, what poet Walt Whitman once described as "not merely a nation, but a teeming Nation of Nations." Between 1820, when the government first began keeping records of their numbers, and 1992, there have been more than sixty million people who have left their native lands to come to the United States. From everywhere on earth they have arrived, looking for better economic prospects, political freedom, and a chance to begin a new life—and bringing their cultures and traditions with them.

Immigration is not only an important part of America, claimed former president John F. Kennedy, it is essential to understanding what America is: "This was the secret of America," he writes, "a nation of people with the fresh memory of old traditions who dared to explore new frontiers, people eager to build lives for themselves in a spacious society that did not restrict their freedom of choice and action."

These words ring true, especially for those immigrants who came to America during the nation's early years. During the first century of its existence, the United States encouraged immigration, for it wanted people to occupy and settle the vast open lands. The nation's first census, taken in 1790, showed a Caucasian population of 3,227,000, and a density of only 4.5 people per square mile! (No one counted or even estimated the numbers of Native Americans, or other racial groups.) Immigrants could come by the shipload, and still the vast continent would accommodate the numbers.

ESTABLISHING LIMITS

Until the late 1800s, in fact, *illegal* immigrant was an unknown concept in the United States. All who arrived were welcome. No guards were stationed at entry points; borders were open and unattended; and people could come and go as they pleased.

There are many reasons why people choose to become immigrants. Most come because of what sociologists call a push-pull factor—elements attract people from other nations to come to the United States, while other elements force them to leave their native lands. Some come because of economic reasons, such as unemployment or poor farming conditions in their own countries. Others leave home because of the promise of freedoms that they had been denied in their native lands.

Congress began restricting immigrants in 1882. The first such restriction was called the Chinese Exclusion Act and was almost totally successful in stopping the large numbers of Chinese immigrants that had started coming into the country during the California gold rush of 1848. Faced with famine, hardship, and social inequality in China, they had been eager to work in a land that promised wealth and opportunity to anyone who worked hard. Almost three hundred thousand Chinese worked in mines, on railroads, and on farms between 1854 and 1883.

But pressure from the public—in large part racially motivated—forced Congress to act to restrict the numbers of Chinese. Many called these immigrants the "Eastern menace" and worried that the Chinese would change the entire social fabric of the nation. Reported the California state legislature in 1876: Chinese immigrants "have never adapted themselves to our habits, mode of dress, or our educational system . . . never ceased the worship of their idol gods, or advanced a step beyond the traditions of their native hive."

RACIAL OVERTONES

Other limitations on immigration in later years were similarly motivated. "It is not to say that some of the fears of the American people were unfounded," says one historian. "There were concerns about jobs, about immigrants working for far less money and thereby stripping power from organized labor. But it is also true that those particular groups being limited were not the groups to which the older immigrants belonged—not the English, the Welsh, the Germans. There were very substantial racist overtones to American immigration policies."

The racist overtones were prevalent when the American people called for more restrictions in the late nineteenth and early twentieth centuries. Millions of immigrants from southern and eastern Europe streamed into the country. They were darker than previous immigrants; their language and their customs were different from what most Americans were used to. The director of the Census Bureau complained that the United States was being overrun by "less desirable immigrants," especially Greeks, Italians, Poles, and Jews, whom he described as "beaten men from beaten races."

The U.S. government again passed legislation that severely limited the numbers of immigrants from certain ethnic groups. Even so, these immigrants continued to come to America, sneaking in by boat, using fake papers, or producing letters documenting them as temporary visitors or students. Legal or illegal, these immigrants had no intention of turning around and going back to the economic and political hardships they had left behind.

UP FROM MEXICO

In the waning years of the twentieth century, illegal immigrants from scores of countries enter the United States. However, the United States seeks to limit the number of Mexican and Central American people crossing over the nineteen hundred-mile-long border between Mexico and the United States. "It's a nightmare," says one INS official, "because no matter how sophisticated our equipment, or how many border patrol officers we place out there, we're fighting a losing battle. For every one we catch, there are probably five or six that get through."

Although the United States has limited Mexican and Central American immigration for many years, we have frequently looked the other way as millions of undocumented people have crossed our borders. "For decades, whenever there was a shortage of farm workers, we pretended we didn't see the Mexican workers coming across the Arizona or New Mexico border," says one INS worker. "They were a ready supply of cheap farm workers, people who'd work for a fraction of the wages that Americans wanted. Employers loved them!"

The Mexican and Central American workers were happy, too. Mexico has long been a poor nation, but rapid population growth and a dramatic decrease in jobs has meant poverty for more and more Mexican people. As one Mexican woman said in disbelief, "I cannot believe how much Americans will pay someone to clean their floors or wash windows! I am pleased to do it."

A COMPLICATED ISSUE

It was this very fact—that the Mexican immigrants were working for less money than American workers demanded—that was both worrying and angering many American workers. And as hundreds of thousands of illegal immigrants were crossing from Mexico into the United States, more and more Americans were becoming frustrated with the government's look-the-other-way attitude. More people meant more crime, they argued, and fewer jobs for citizens.

"They take our jobs, they move into our cities and cause overcrowding," complains one man from Los Angeles. Other people complain about the large numbers of illegal immigrants, claiming that the Mexican and Central American immigrants bring crime, drugs, and health problems with them. "Why should we as taxpayers support them when they aren't even Americans?"asks one Chicago woman. "Why should they get benefits, such as free public education and so on, that should be reserved for U.S. citizens?"

Such thinking angers many illegal immigrants. They deny that they are taking American jobs, citing the fact that no Americans apply for the jobs they do—usually minimum-wage work such as cleaning and boring factory work.

They say, too, that the restrictions the United States puts on immigrants seem random, based on nothing but politics. "It makes me mad," says one Tijuana man. "My parents and my older sisters came here, no problem, six years ago. Border officials didn't care *who* walked across. Then all of a sudden, the borders are tight, lots of security. Why would they be glad for my parents and sisters to come, and all of a sudden, me and my wife and little boy are unwanted?"

One woman from a rural town in Mexico says that she feels bad breaking a law in the United States, but she feels she had very little choice in coming to California from the poverty back in Mexico. "Sometimes you Americans forget how lucky you are, how many choices you have," she says. "For you, you think of options like 'Do I buy this dress or should I buy that one?' or 'Will we buy that blue car or this yellow one?' For many of us in Mexico, it was choices like 'Does our family eat breakfast today or not?' or 'Can we afford to let our two small children go to school, or should we have them work in the fields?' Those are the choices for many of us. It is a matter of survival for my children and for me."

Other illegal immigrants point to the dangers they must face in coming to America, risking their very lives. If it were not a crucial matter for them, they say, they would never put their lives and the lives of their families in such danger. "You can die being shot by a guard or being robbed and beaten by the coyote [smuggler] you hire to bring you in," says one man. "It's not easy to get in, and once you're in, there's no guarantee that you won't get picked up and sent back. There is nothing frivolous about what we are doing."

QUESTIONS ARISING

In recent months the issue of immigration has become a hot political topic, especially in states like Texas, California, and Arizona, where many illegal immigrants live and work. And questions keep arising, questions that evoke emotional answers from both sides.

For instance, some Americans favor tight immigration control and urge the government to allocate more money for security at our borders. They claim that the influx of Mexican and Central American immigrants could prove harmful to the culture and way of life that Americans have attained. They believe that adding in the large numbers of illegal immigrants might prove disastrous. "One doesn't wish to be unkind," writes one critic of immigration, "but cultural pluralism [diversity] is not the most attractive legacy we can leave our children."

On the other hand, some argue that, unlike many other nations, the United States has never had a national culture, and that an increase in different customs, languages, and ideas can only add freshness to a culturally diverse society. The alternative, they say, is stagnancy, which would be a deathblow to American society. "Cultures and societies, like living organisms, need food from outside in order to grow and survive," claims one writer. "And, like every living organism, the moment they cease changing they begin to die."

Some critics of immigration worry about the effect of so many unskilled workers on the U.S. economy. "I got nothing against Mexicans personally," says one factory worker from St. Paul, Minnesota, "but I don't want them—especially the illegal ones—taking jobs away from me or from my kids. They got no more right grabbing jobs away from American workers than I've got going to Mexico and taking one of their jobs."

But there are others who dispute the idea that immigrants are bad for the American economy. "They earn money, they spend money," writes one economist. "They have money deducted from their earnings that pays for social security and the illegal immigrants can't even draw from that money. How does that hurt native-born Americans? The last study I saw was that immigrants are paying in $90 billion in taxes in this country!" Many who employ unskilled illegal immigrants agree: "People moan about how the immigrants are taking jobs, but I can't find Americans who will work on my farms. It's hard work, and lots of people work a week and say, 'That's it, I've had enough.' It's easier to collect welfare, I guess. Give me an immigrant worker any day."

BEYOND BEING A "PROBLEM"

The Other America: Illegal Immigrants offers no answers, easy or otherwise, to such questions. It is the people and their own stories, rather than the issues, that are presented here. And although many of their circumstances were similar before they came to the United States, their individual stories are very different.

Alicia is a young mother whose husband has been apprehended and sent back to Mexico. She worries about the neighborhood in which she and her children must live, since they can no longer afford the nice home they had before her husband's arrest. Manuel, a single man in his forties, has been in the United States for many years but has not broken out of a cycle of poverty. Carolina is a Mexican woman who has had to learn about injustice and bigotry in her factory job. And Jose and Maria, grandparents from El Salvador, came to the United States after the civil war in their native land claimed the lives of two of their sons.

Reading their stories should make anyone who is concerned about the "issue" or "problem" of illegal immigrants see things in a somewhat more personal light. As with other segments of society presented in *The Other America* series, there are vivid names and faces attached to the issue, and their perspective is a valuable tool in completely understanding the scope of the topic.

Alicia

"I HOPE THAT PEOPLE
UNDERSTAND THAT MOST OF US
ARE GOOD PEOPLE. MOST OF US
LOVE THE LIFE HERE; WE WANT
TO FIT IN, WORK, AND PAY TAXES.
WE WANT . . . TO LIVE WITHOUT
CRIME, WITHOUT FEAR. IS NOT
THAT THE SAME AS MOST
AMERICANS?"

The area is almost a stereotype of what inner-city life is becoming, with garbage strewn about, people listlessly draped on bus stop benches, leaning against fences. A crack dealer in baggy pants and a blue bandanna seems to be doing a thriving business among four-teen- and fifteen-year olds who should be in school. And there is the deep thrum of electric bass coming from ever-present car stereos.

Alicia answers the door to the white apartment building ner-vously, as if she is unsure whether to let the strangers in. She speaks almost no English and is relieved that one of the visitors is bilingual. The interpreter greets Alicia, assuring her that the visi-tors are not connected in any way with the Immigration and Natu-ralization Service (INS), the governmental agency that often arrests immigrants who are in the United States illegally. She lis-tens intently, asking questions and glancing outside to make cer-tain there are no government cars.

At last convinced that her visitors pose no threat, Alicia leads the way to an upstairs apartment, which is a sharp contrast to the ac-tivities and litter outside. It is airy and colorful, with paintings and posters on the walls. Although she has four children, there are no

Alicia's son wrestles on his bedroom floor with a friend. Alicia's four children spend most of their free time inside the apartment because they live in a dangerous neighborhood.

shoes or toys cluttering the living room, no clothing strewn around. The only sign of children, in fact, is the bright pictures hanging on the refrigerator that the younger ones have brought home from school. The wood floors gleam; the counters are immaculate.

How does she keep such a neat home with four young children living here? Alicia gives a pleased smile.

"They spend a lot of time inside when they come home from school," she says. "And there is not much for them to do inside except do their homework and help me clean! You see, this neighborhood is very bad, very bad. You can take a look outside and see the gangs; you can hear all the bad language, all the noise. Too many things that are dangerous for children. I rarely let them outside, unless my oldest son, Luis, 13, is with them, but even then I worry."

"IT WAS NOT THAT I HATED MEXICO"

Alicia, her husband, Jose, and their four children have come to the United States from Mexico. Because they have no papers entitling them to work and live here, they are considered illegal.

"My relatives are all here in the United States," she says. "I have four brothers and four sisters, and they are all here legally. They arrived before we did, at a time when it was easier to get papers making an immigrant legal. My father is an American citizen now, and that makes him very proud!

"I think it is hard for some Americans to understand why people like me come to the United States. It was not that I hated Mexico. In fact, I miss it very much. But it is impossible for most Mexicans to be anything except poor. In Mexico you can work hard but not make enough money to buy food for your family or to fix your house.

"In Mexico there is so much poverty and so much corruption. It is actually a rich land, because there are many resources there, like tin, silver, things like that. But it is not Mexico's people who benefit from the sale of the resources—only the few wealthy, that's who gets rich. The majority of the people, they have no return on [income from] any of that business. So therefore, many of the poor Mexican people dream of coming to the United States to get a job and earn some money—lots more than they could ever earn in Mexico!"

"A Beautiful Childhood"

Alicia stresses that even without much money, her own childhood in Mexico was very pleasant.

"I think of it as a beautiful childhood," she says with a smile. "As I said before, I had eight brothers and sisters, so there was always lots of talking, lots of laughing. We had fun together after school, jumping rope and playing hide and seek. We went swimming in the river near our house. We didn't even need extra friends, for there were so many of us!

"My mother was a homemaker; my father was a merchant. He had a clothing store. I didn't think of us as rich or poor. We always had enough to eat, so in that way we were luckier than many other people."

Alicia became pregnant when she was in tenth grade—not unusual at all in Mexico, she says—and married.

"Jose was very handsome, and a hard worker," she remembers. "He was only sixteen, a year older than I was, but he was already learning to be an electrician. He had been studying that trade since he was thirteen. That was the Mexican way, to learn a trade early, starting as an apprentice to someone older. Very often boys started in their father's footsteps. Jose did that, too. Since his father was in construction, he had many contacts with electricians and other laborers that could help his son. So by the time Jose and I married, he had a three-year start on his career. We were looking forward to having a happy life together, raising children."

"WONDERFUL STORIES ABOUT THE UNITED STATES"

Within several years Alicia and Jose had four small children. Although they both worked hard, she taking care of the home and he at his electrician's job, they were not able to make ends meet.

"Jose's job depended so much on the economy," she explains. "People who are not building houses do not need electricians. Neither do businesses that are not expanding, or apartment buildings that are not going up. The shortage of good jobs meant less money for people, and that in turn meant less work for Jose and other workers like him.

"My own father was feeling the strain, too. His clothing shop was not going well, and he decided that it was best for them to move. They went to the United States and started new lives there. But Jose and I were not ready to leave yet. We said we were busy with our small children but that we would join them eventually. We promised we would meet up with them later, when we were ready to make the move."

Alicia says that it was difficult for her when her parents and brothers and sisters left. Not having the support of a family seemed almost unbearable.

"It had gone on eight years," she says. "I missed them so. You need to talk to people who know you, who care about you. You cannot talk to a stranger about personal things, after all! We wrote letters back and forth, and that helped a little. Their letters were filled with wonderful stories about the United States and what a wonderful place it was to live. They said, 'Alicia, you must come up here soon.'"

PREPARING TO LEAVE

As their financial situation continued to worsen, Alicia and Jose knew that it was time to leave for the United States. It was decided that Jose would go first, to find a job and a place for the family to live. When he could accumulate enough money, he would send for her.

"He wanted to make fifteen hundred dollars at least," she says. "We knew that the best way for me and the children to get across the border was to hire what we called a coyote—a man who makes his living by sneaking others across the Mexican border into the United States. And fifteen hundred dollars was what he would charge. At first I thought that was far too much money, but Jose told me no, I should not worry about spending the money. Once we were safely in the United States, we could earn the money back quickly.

"We had heard that some of the coyotes were bad; some would take money and not help you at all. But this man was recommended, and Jose knew we could trust him to help me and the children across. And so Jose got settled, not too far from where my family was living. He got odd jobs, working at whatever temporary job he could get, and sent me money. And it wasn't too long before I had enough to hire the coyote.

"I sold most of our belongings because I knew we would not be able to take anything with us—a few clothes, our birth certificates, nothing more than that. It was difficult, too. Leaving any home behind is hard."

"EVERYWHERE THE SMUGGLERS"

Alicia and her children, ages ten, seven, six, and four, traveled from their home in Guadalajara to Tijuana, a city in northern Mexico not far from the California border. There they met up with their coyote. As Jose had instructed her, she paid his fee right away, before the border crossing. There was no credit in such situations, Jose had said.

"I was so surprised at how many people in Tijuana were there doing the same thing we were going to do," she says. "Many families with children, old people, young people. And everywhere the smugglers, the coyotes, willing to smuggle anyone across for a fee."

The smuggler Alicia had hired explained the plan. She and her children were to stay in a nearby motel, as if they were vacationers. They would spend the next afternoon at the beach, like tourists. "We were supposed to wait until very late there at the beach," she explains, "and then we would cross from Tijuana to San Diego, California, just to the north. There were others—maybe

Alicia and her family fled Mexico because of its poverty and corrupt government. "In Mexico," Alicia says, "you can work hard but not make enough money to buy food for your family or to fix your house."

forty or fifty—who were going to be doing the same thing that night. The crossing was going to be difficult, because we would be walking through water, a shallow lake, the whole way.

"I had talked with my children, told them how important it was that they were very quiet. I said that there were soldiers and police who were watching for people like us, so we could not make any noise. Luis, my oldest son, was very good about talking to the younger ones and helping me explain to them. I also told them all that even though they were old enough to walk alone, the coyote and I would carry them. The coyote was very firm about this; he did not want to take a chance that the children would be too sleepy and slow, for they might get separated from us."

Alicia says that as the time got later, she found herself getting more and more nervous.

"I was nervous about my children mostly," she says. "I worried that they would be lost or be taken from me. I told myself, it will soon be over, and we will be over the border. I looked around at all those people. I thought about my family, too. I thought, if they can all do this thing, surely me and my children can, too!"

"RAPIDO, RAPIDO!"

When darkness finally came to the beach at Tijuana, Alicia and her children began walking north, toward the shallow lake and channel that separated Tijuana from San Diego.

"Just as I expected, there were others walking, too," she explains. "Many were carrying children. It was very quiet, for no one wanted to attract the attention of the border patrol. We knew they were out there, but it was so dark, we hoped that they would not see us. We just kept following the precautions we'd been given: to stay together, keep quiet, not even a whisper. Everything had to be organized just so, so that the border patrol wouldn't hear us. And I prayed to God that he would get us across safely.

"It is hard for me to remember how many miles, or kilometers, that we walked that night. I was so worried, I was concentrating on just walking, keeping my children quiet. I carried two, the smuggler carried two. We walked for over an hour, maybe two. It was slow going, through that water.

"That was the hardest part. The coyote kept saying, 'Rapido, rapido!' to keep us moving faster and faster. It was maybe two o'clock in the morning, and we could see the lights of the city getting closer and closer. It seemed that we were going to make it, until my daughter, Sandra, got excited and spoke."

Alicia shakes her head, smiling. She says that it was difficult to be angry, for her daughter was so young.

"We all heard a noise behind us, and we were frightened. It was the border patrol. Would they realize we were there? Sandra got excited. She said, 'Oh, Mama, there is someone there, someone there!' She was trying to warn us, and she forgot the first rule: be silent. Yes, there was someone, and the someone heard her and found us."

CAUGHT, AND TWO MORE TRIES

Alicia says that her daughter was instantly sorry for her mistake, but nothing could be done to correct it.

"She felt so badly, for she was only seven. She cried and cried, because it was her fault, even though we did not blame her. Another woman and her two children were caught with us, too. They had been walking right next to us. The coyote did not get caught; he knew how to run away quickly and hide. You see, the smugglers do not want to be caught and charged, because what they were doing is a federal crime. They would go to prison, for certain."

Alicia says that they were taken by the border patrol to the American immigration service, where officers put her in an area that she calls *cordalon*, a holding area for all the illegal immigrants that had been caught in the area.

"It was not a nice place," she remembers. "It was loud and dirty, and there was nowhere to sit or be comfortable. There were armed guards there, patrolling the *cordalon*. They were not mean. In fact they laughed at me, so young with four children. They said, 'You and your husband obviously do not have television—something to do with your time at night!" She laughs shyly, remembering.

"They took us by bus then, and sent us back across the border to Tijuana, where I met up with our coyote. No, I didn't have to give him any more money. That fifteen hundred dollars was payment for as many times as we needed to try to get across the border. And we did try again, that very same night. That wasn't successful either, but the following night we were successful. I was glad, because I had told the children, 'If we don't get across tonight, we're going home to Guadalajara!'"

SAFE HOUSES, BACK ALLEYS, AND FREEDOM

The crossing of the border that night was without incident, says Alicia, and when she and her children got to San Diego, they went with the smuggler to some apartment buildings eight blocks away.

"We walked in between some buildings, through a back alley," she says, "and there was a car waiting for us there. It took us to a safe house not too far from there so we could change our wet clothes and rest for a little while. After a while the coyote woke us and told us it was time to go to the airport, where there was a plane that would take us to San Francisco. From there, we would be on our own. That was a scary part for me, because when we were given these instructions, the coyote told us, 'If you get caught, remember you don't know me. Memorize my phone number, but don't write it down. And *never* call me if you are caught!' It was very involved, very organized, and there were lots of steps to the whole process. That is why it cost us so much money. The coyote was well paid, but he had to earn his money!"

21

"WHAT A CELEBRATION WE HAD!"

Once in San Francisco, Alicia allowed herself to relax. She called Jose long distance and told him she and the children were safely across the border.

"I waited for him for fifteen days," she says. "He and my father made arrangements to borrow a car, and they drove out to California to pick us up. It was a little car, a Grand Am, I think they called it. It seemed to take them such a long time. I was so anxious to see them so I would know for sure that we were together as a family again!

"The children and I were so excited when they arrived. And what a ride home we had! Seven of us in that little car—Jose and my father in the front, me and the children squashed into the back. But they were so happy [that] there was no shoving, no cross words. The children were so happy to see their father once again."

Alicia says that Jose and her father had stopped at a supermarket in San Francisco and had purchased a lot of supplies so they would not have to spend much money on the ride home.

"We had ham, oranges, bread, apples, cheese—it was like a banquet!" she remembers. "All the things we would need. I slept a lot in that back seat; I think I was just relieved that the worrying and anxiety were over for us.

"And when we arrived in our new U.S. home, what a celebration we had! Everyone had gathered to greet us—my brothers and sisters and their families, and little nieces and nephews born in the past several years that I had not even met yet. It was a grand party. We laughed, and cried, and hugged, and did we ever eat!"

A NEW LIFE

At this point in her story, two small boys in jeans and T-shirts creep silently into the kitchen. They wave shyly at the visitors and smile. Alicia speaks rapidly to them in Spanish, but the two answer in English, never taking their eyes off the guests at the kitchen table.

"So you want something to eat?" she asks. To the guests, she announces, "This is my youngest son and his friend. My little one here, he missed the bus this morning for school. He is not supposed to be home, but he was so sleepy this morning I guess he could not keep up with his brother and sisters."

She ruffles his hair. "Take an orange and go back into your room. Why don't you listen to records or dance, you two?"

Handing each boy an orange and a napkin, Alicia sinks back into her chair. Soon the sounds of a Gloria Estefan record can be heard coming from the bedroom, followed by bumps and giggles.

"Our new life here in America has been good, mostly," she says. "Right away, I noticed what a difference there was in working here and working in Mexico. The first twelve years of our married life, with Jose working so hard, we could afford very little. We had a small house that we were building ourselves from scratch, and we were able to buy a refrigerator and a tiny television. That is, by sacrificing and doing without other things. And that was after working hard for twelve years!

"Here, though, things are very different. In a year and a half here, we had a nice place to live (not where we live now), some furniture, a color television, and a used car. We have bought furniture and other nice things for our home. We live simply, as you can see, but it is luxury compared to how we were living in Mexico."

Alicia says that they would be even better off financially if their immigrant status had changed from illegal to legal.

"Jose has not been able to work as an electrician since coming here," she says with disappointment. "You see, an electrician here must be licensed, and Jose cannot fill out papers to become licensed; the information they ask would give him away. He has only fake papers, ones that he bought from someone when he first came here. So he has been working at odd jobs: housekeeping, maintenance work, painting, working at fast-food places, things like that. He cannot work long, for the longer he works at one place, the more likely that the INS or someone will discover that his papers are not real and catch up to him."

CAUGHT

Alicia maintains that the only bad part of their new life has been the fear and uncertainty, the worrying about whether they will be discovered as illegals in the United States. For Jose, she says sadly, that has just happened.

"It was only a few weeks ago that he was sent back to Mexico," she says. "The whole thing happened as an accident; he was stopped by the police as he drove to work at his night job, because

After Jose was deported to Mexico, hard times fell on Alicia and her family. They were forced to move to their current apartment, which is less expensive but is located in a high crime neighborhood.

he had a broken headlight. When the police stopped him, they found on their computer that he had not made a court appearance the year before, and so he was arrested and taken into custody."

Why had he been summoned to court? Alicia shrugs.

"It was for a traffic accident, one in which he was not to blame. But he was supposed to be a witness, and he did not come. So that stayed on his record. I think he didn't show up at court because he worried that if the people in court asked him a lot of questions, they might find out that the work papers he was using were not real.

"He went to a judge, who realized Jose was illegal. From there he was turned over to INS, who came to where he worked and took him. He barely had time to say good-bye to us before he was sent to a detention center for a while, then sent to Laredo, Texas, and from there sent by plane to Guadalajara."

Surprisingly enough, she says, the INS does not necessarily send every illegal immigrant immediately back across the border. In fact, Jose had been detained a year before and had been allowed to remain.

"We think that someone fingered him [the first time]," she says. "Someone reported him, and he was questioned by the INS. But they gave him a break, since he told them he had already filed for papers that would make him legal. That process, though, can take many months, and the INS people knew that. They told him to work hard on getting his papers, and they allowed him to stay.

"In some ways, it makes sense for the INS to be lenient with some of us. It costs the U.S. government money every time they detain someone: for food, for the detention camp, for the airplane flight back to Mexico. And if someone is working hard, trying to become legal, trying to raise a family, why force them out? Especially when they will probably come back soon, anyway! But Jose should have taken advantage of the time they gave him. He made a mistake in not using that second chance. He should have talked to a lawyer and worked harder to get a card enabling him to work. It is too bad, but that's how it happened."

HARD TIMES

When Jose was sent back to Mexico, the family's luck changed dramatically. Alicia and her children could not afford to live in the same university neighborhood as when Jose was working, so they were forced to move.

"It was very sad for us," she says. "Jose was the one with the jobs; my job was to keep the house, make sure the children were happy. But without the money he brought in, we are very poor. We cannot stay in our other home, where the people were friendly and it was safe for the children to play outside.

"Here there are gangs everywhere, and drug dealers, too. The police sirens are loud all night and all day. My little ones want to go outside when they can play, but I don't feel right sending them out, even with Luis or Sandra. Luis is lucky, because a friend from school got him a tryout with a good soccer team to play on, and he has done well. He has always loved soccer. His father is a good soccer player, too. The coach of this good team is willing to pick him up for practices and games, so Luis is happy that he has something fun to do. It is the other children that I feel sorry for.

"My hope is that this is only temporary. Jose has already written to me, saying that he is in touch with a man who can help him get a work permit so that he can be working here while we wait for the papers that will give him legal status. But who knows how

Alicia's son Luis (left) watches his teammates from the sidelines during one of his soccer games.

long it will take that man to get a work permit for Jose? Maybe three months, or maybe longer! We hope it is not that long before he can come back to us."

"I FEEL GRATEFUL FOR MANY THINGS"

What money does she and the children live on, now that Jose is back in Mexico? Alicia shrugs and smiles.

"I get no welfare for myself," she says. "There is no money from the federal government that takes care of me or the children—no food stamps or things like that. But this state does help out with relief for my children. Each state is different, but this one is good; it is very generous. I have five hundred dollars each month to pay for food and rent for us.

"But it is not much, as you can see. We live in a bad place. There is a free clinic not far from here if the children get sick. For me, though, I worry. There is nothing to help me if I become hurt or sick, so I pray that I do not! I try to be optimistic, though, and to be grateful for what I do have. I feel grateful for many things, for the fact that we are better off here—even as poor as we are— than we were back in Mexico. I am grateful that my children have a nice school to go to, where they have teachers that help them learn. I am grateful also that our family is healthy, and except for Jose, [that] we are all together still."

Asked if she ever feels guilty when she considers that she is breaking the law by being in this country illegally, she shakes her head vehemently.

"People here do not always understand," she says, no longer smiling. "My children now are part of a fifth generation of immigrants who have come to this country. My great-grandfather did it, my grandfather, my father, my brothers and sisters and me, and my children. All the ones before us had the opportunity, and they took it.

"Now, how come they can be Americans, become citizens, like my father has, and yet Jose and I are not welcome here? Why are we all of a sudden breaking a law, when all we do is what our relatives have done legally? It makes no sense to me. We are good people; we are willing to come here, work hard, raise good children. But all of a sudden the times are different. While in other years immigrants from Mexico were welcomed with open arms, suddenly things are different."

"I Am Not a Criminal"

There is a wrong assumption about Mexicans who cross over the borders illegally, she says, and that bothers her.

"Most of the people who come here from Mexico are workers," she says. "They know that there are jobs here that many American workers won't do. It is not that we do those jobs better, it's that we will do the jobs, period. Do you need vegetables harvested? Does the fruit need to be picked? Are there menial jobs that must be done, and no one wants to do them?

"In a way, we are doing the Americans a favor; that is how I sometimes look at it. I am not a criminal, Jose is not a criminal. We are not drug smugglers or thieves or murderers. We come here to work, to raise our families. We do not worry about getting dirty when we work, or sweating."

And the recent tightening of immigration laws that makes it more difficult for immigrants from Mexico and Central America to get jobs in the United States? She purses her lips, thinking.

"I think that it is politics, what is going on. And it is sort of two-faced of the government to play games with people. Sometimes we are welcome, sometimes we are not. My grandfather is welcome, my children are not. They will tighten regulations, they will loosen them. It is not based on what is real; that is what I think.

"What *is* real is the way employers are glad to hire Jose and other immigrants. They don't look too hard at the papers the men show them. They maybe suspect that they are not legal, but they don't ask. The fake IDs, the fake work permits—they don't ask because they don't really want to know. And the reason is exactly what I say: they know those men will work willingly. They will work harder than others for the money, and even for less money!"

Alicia concedes that many stereotypes have their roots in something that is true, and she knows that some immigrants have not been good additions to the U.S. population.

"There are some, yes, who are not always good people. But that is true everywhere; no culture or country has all good people. There are good people and bad. Some who are honest and fair, others who make trouble. And it is as true with immigrants as it is with any group. There are some who sell drugs, some who come here and do not work, who get on welfare and are lazy. But do not make me and my children pay for the sins of other people!

"Those who are bad are not the majority. I hope that people understand that most of us are good people. Most of us love the life here; we want to fit in, work, and pay taxes. We worry about our children, like all mothers and fathers. We want the best for our families. We want to live without crime, without fear. Is not that the same as most Americans?"

WORRIES

As grateful as she is about her life here, Alicia says that there are aspects of her life that she worries about.

"I feel that we are trapped here in this neighborhood," she says. "Not just that we cannot move away, but that it is difficult for us to go anywhere, to travel around the city. We have a car—at least we own one. It is Jose's, but it is still back in our old neighborhood, being looked after by a man who was once our neighbor.

"I cannot drive it. Even if I had a license, I wouldn't know how," she says with a laugh. "I'm sure I would hit a bus or a tree! So until Jose is here, we are stuck here. Occasionally we take a bus, but it is expensive and difficult with the little ones, especially if Luis and Sandra are not with me."

Alicia says that because she does not work or drive, it is difficult for her to make friendships. She admits that it can be quite
lonely, especially with her husband away for an indefinite period
of time.

"When Jose was here, he played soccer at the park near our old
house," she remembers. "There was a men's league that played on
Sunday afternoons, and the teams were very good, very exciting to
watch. I would take the children, and we would watch the games.
That was a good way to meet other people. I got to be friends with
some of the other team members and their wives. There were two
of the players who were from Ecuador and another couple from
the Dominican Republic. But I do not see them anymore.

"I also know that because I cannot speak English, it is hard for
me to meet new people. That is a goal of mine: eventually I would
like to go to classes like Jose did to learn to speak it and understand. But with the children so small, it is hard for me to get away
by myself to do that. I would not want to leave them alone, not in
this neighborhood. It would not be right."

*Life in the United States is often lonely for Alicia. In addition to missing her
husband, she says it is difficult for her to meet new people when she cannot
speak English.*

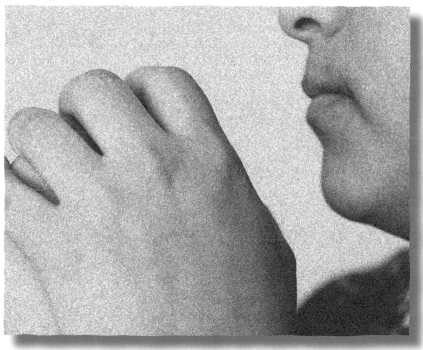

Always a Worry

Is part of her isolation based on fear that she and her children might be caught by the INS? Alicia nods tensely. That is a worry that does not go away, she says.

"When the INS took Jose away, the children were very upset," she says. "They could remember how excited they had been when they and I came to the United States and when they saw their father again. And now, for him to be back in Mexico, they are worried, yes.

"The children are all aware of the fact that we are illegal here. There are no secrets in our family; it is not right to keep that from them. They know that they must answer 'yes' if someone asks them if they are legal immigrants. A lie? Yes, I suppose so, but it is necessary for our family to survive together. And it is not a lie in one way, for Jose is working hard to make sure we become legal. We will someday have our documents.

"I must be positive and optimistic. Nothing good comes of worrying, of thinking bad thoughts. Is it in my mind? All of the time, yes. I think about the children at school and wonder if one of the children will mention their father being sent back. I think about someone just making a random search, looking for anyone who looks Mexican, asking to see papers. Just like Jose, a chance encounter with a policeman, over something as routine as a broken light on a car. But I must try not to worry, I know that."

Between Two Cultures

Another thing that occupies Alicia's thoughts is the difficulties of raising Mexican children in this new place. It is, she maintains, like being caught between two cultures sometimes.

"There is a big difference, I think, in how children are raised in Mexico and how they are raised here," she says thoughtfully. "In some ways I feel torn apart, because I feel as though my children are moving away from me, moving away from Mexican ways.

"Back home in Guadalajara children were taught to respect their elders in the way they talked, in their actions. It wasn't unusual to see young people honoring older people. It was just the way things were there. Those traditions just run deeper in Mexico, I think, than they do here.

"Now that we are here, I do not see that same respect in my two older children. I worry that they are losing respect for older people, for traditions. I do not like to see that in my children, because I know they are good children, very good.

"Luis is the one I worry most about, since he is the oldest—a teenager of thirteen. He is torn in two ways, too, wanting to be a tough boy and at the same time wanting to be a good son, obeying his traditions and his family."

Alicia waves her hands helplessly in the air, as if she is very frustrated.

"This morning I get a call from Luis's school," she says, "and they tell me that he is going to be suspended from his eighth-grade class. For three days! He got into a fight on the playground, the principal told me, and he must stay home now, miss school. Luis was angry. It had something to do with baseball, I think. One boy was out, but said that he wasn't, and Luis settled it with his fists.

"A silly thing, a wrong thing to fight about. It was not important, but for me to say that to Luis is impossible. To him, anything involved with sports seems important. It is life or death, or so it

Sitting on the sidewalk, Alicia's children eagerly watch a Cinco de Mayo parade. Alicia worries that her children will forget their Mexican heritage. "I feel as though my children are moving away from me, moving away from Mexican ways," she confides.

seems. Back home in Mexico, I could spank a little boy who doesn't listen. But here, spanking is considered bad. The children are looked at as higher up, more important than old people. No one can hurt them—even for a minute, even for their own good—to learn something. That makes it harder, in my opinion."

She sighs, looking wistful. "In my opinion, yes."

"I HAVE GOALS"

Alicia stands up quickly and begins clearing the coffee things from the kitchen table.

"It is almost time for the children to come home," she says. "I need to make a snack for them so they can begin their homework when they come in. I know Luis will be angry, because he'll have spent this afternoon in the principal's office."

It is clear that she wants to spend no more time thinking about her family's immigration status; there is food to be prepared and the dishes to do.

"I enjoy talking," she says with a shy smile, "but sometimes I feel that there is so little I can say. My life is not moving forward right now. It will soon, I hope, as soon as Jose comes back to us. Luis will not be so restless and worried, and our family will have money once again.

"I have goals, but they are quite simple. I don't need to be rich; things like that don't interest me much. But to have enough to move back to the place we had near the university—that would be enough. And to be able to live in this country without worrying about the INS, or being sent home.

"I want my children to become smart and able to work. I don't want them to forget how to speak Spanish, no matter how good they are becoming at English. I want a yard for the young ones to play in. And maybe learn to drive that silly car, to go visiting if I make a friend!"

Manuel

"SURE, I DO LIKE THAT
FANTASY . . . BEING RICH, MAKING
MONEY, HAVING A BIG HOUSE,
AND A PRETTY CAR TO DRIVE
AROUND. BUT THOSE ARE JUST
DREAMS. I KNOW THIS IS THE
LAND OF OPPORTUNITIES,
BUT . . . THE FANTASY IS NOT
GOING TO HAPPEN FOR ME."

Manuel, in his forties, is a small, stocky man in soiled work clothes and a bright blue baseball cap. His T-shirt bears the name of a pricey lakefront restaurant frequented by the city's young singles. It is not surprising when he says he did not purchase the shirt himself.

"It is very surprising to me what people are willing to give away," he says, pointing to the shirt. "I found this outside a house yesterday morning, in a bag of things on the curb. I don't know why anyone would ever need to buy clothes with things like this sitting there free."

Manuel claims that he gets almost all of his clothing this way, from looking through give-away bags and trash barrels. Everything—even shoes—can be obtained if one only takes the time to rummage a little, he says with a shrug.

He is clearly uncomfortable in the confines of his chair. He does not mind being interviewed, he says, only he is not sure who would ever want to read about anything he would have to say! Making a minute adjustment to the brim of his hat, he coughs and tries to get more comfortable on his chair. This done, he stares intently at his hands in his lap. When he finally begins to talk, it is with a low, singsong voice.

"I don't mind speaking English; I don't like interpreters," he adds, glaring at the interpreter who has offered his services. "I think sometimes they get my words wrong. Besides, I like to practice my English. That is the language I've got to speak, since I live here now, right?"

ON PROBATION

Manuel is from Mexico and has been in the United States for almost fourteen years. His goal has been to become legal in this country, although, he says with a great deal of embarrassment, his plans have been delayed.

"I'm on probation," he says, staring down at his hands in his lap. "For ten years. I was angry at my girlfriend, and I lost my temper. She made me mad because I thought she cared only for me, but it turned out that she was seeing another man. I got jealous, and I pushed her. Her glasses broke, and I got into trouble.

"I know without anybody telling me that that was a bad thing to do. When she called the police and I had to go to court, the judge scolded me. He said, 'Why do you come from Mexico to the United States to do something like this? Why do you push a lady you say you love? What are you thinking about, Manuel?' He was right; I have no reason to do something like that. I was jealous, but that wasn't good for me to be that way."

Manuel shakes his head. "I went to jail for a little time, only six months. But that was too long, because while I was in the jail, I missed an important appointment. I was supposed to see a government worker about getting my legal papers so I can be here in this country. Now I've got to wait until my probation is through, another four years. Then I can start over, getting those papers."

Manuel says he is angry, mostly at himself. He explains that he was stupid and crazy to have let himself get into trouble like this.

"This wasn't how I wanted to be," he says. "I was trying to do things right, do what I planned to do. I am a Mexican, here in the United States. I should be working hard at a job, making money, right? The United States is good, I know, since there is money here for people who want to work hard. That's me. I like to work hard, make money.

Manuel immigrated to the United States nearly fourteen years ago. Although he had hoped to work hard and become wealthy, Manuel says he soon discovered that the American dream was out of reach.

"But why am I sitting in jail, when I should be working? That was crazy. So I will never do that again. I will not see that lady anymore; I will go on with my life and have good behavior so that I can become legal here."

"THE FANTASY IS NOT GOING TO HAPPEN FOR ME"

There are many people in Mexico, says Manuel, who fantasize about coming to the United States and becoming wealthy. They see how plentiful jobs are here and how much higher wages are. However, he says, it's important for them to understand that most immigrants from Mexico will never achieve those dreams.

"Most of them are like me," he says. "I am not well educated. I managed to get here across the border, so that is something. But I am not successful. Sure, I do like that fantasy, you know? Being rich, making money, having a big house, and a pretty car to drive around. I sometimes even do that now, think about what I could become. But those are just dreams. I know this is the land of opportunities, but those are not for me. The fantasy is not going to happen for me.

"Why? Well, first of all, look at my color. I am brown. It's harder for people with color to be successful. Not impossible, but harder. And second, the English. When you come here, you must speak good English, not sound like a Mexican or someone who doesn't belong here. And I do try, but I don't do it so good yet.

"To have that fantasy happen, you need a good job. It isn't enough to work hard. You have to have a job that can make lots of money. Look at me. I come here, I work hard, but what am I doing with my days? I am washing windows, cleaning the bathrooms. That is not good. I mean, those things have to be done; people all want clean windows and clean bathrooms. But that is not how you make the money to make your fantasies come true!"

Manuel says he knows that education is important, and that is the one thing that many Mexican immigrants lack.

"Most Mexicans who come here, they come for change. Most of us don't have a good education. We start out at the schools, but we leave and don't finish. It is not too often that regular people in Mexico even go to high school. No one I know went to college; that is for people who have lots of money, not me. You need to go to school not just to learn how to do things, but to make good decisions. That is what I haven't done, you see. I don't make good decisions."

AN UNSETTLED UPBRINGING

Manuel's childhood in Mexico can at least partially explain the decision-making difficulties he has as an adult. He was raised in a very poor family. His mother was a waitress in a restaurant; his father worked only sporadically, instead spending most of his day drinking.

"My mother made the money for us," he says. "There was my sister and me, we were the only children. My mother didn't make much, but she spent what she had on sending me to a good school. It was a school boys go to, who maybe will become priests someday. The classes are good, lots of things to learn. I was six when I went to live at that school.

"I was not excited to leave. I cried—I remember that. I wanted to stay home. I remember asking my mother why did I have to leave, why couldn't I go to the same school as my sister went to. My mother told me that she wanted me to turn out better than my father. She said, 'Manuel, look at your father, how all he does is drink and make trouble. I don't want my son to grow up like that. You go to school and learn and make something good out of your-self. Even if you don't become a holy father, you can learn a lot, get a good job when you are a man.' So, I went."

A TRAGIC STORY

Manuel says that he saw his mother only once in the nine years he attended that school, because it was far from their home. When she came to visit him, it was to inform him that his father had died.

"It was very strange for me," he says. "She came to me and said, 'Manuel, I have something to tell you. Your father, he died. He was shot by the border patrol.' It didn't seem real to me, what she was saying. She said, 'Manuel, you are going to have a new fa-ther.' I said 'Okay,' because I didn't know what else to say. I can be honest, and say that I wasn't going to cry about my father, because we were not very close. For me, it was okay, I think. I didn't really think one way or the other."

She explained what had happened, though, in more detail. It was not because his father was attempting to escape or to sneak across the border that he was shot. Instead, his father was shot in the act of beating his wife.

"She and my father had been trying to pass [legally] over the border," he explains. "My mother had no trouble crossing; she was very light skinned. She was Spanish, rather than part Indian like so many Mexican people. I'm convinced that's why she crossed real easy. But my father, he was detained. And that made him mad, real mad.

"You know," says Manuel, "lots of Mexican men are very jealous, get mad real easy. My father was like that; he was very possessive of her. And while she was over the border for two weeks, he stayed there and waited for her. As time went on, he became real suspicious, like maybe something was going on—maybe she had a boyfriend or something. I don't know . . . that's just the way he thought. My uncle is that way too. He told me once that when his wife was a couple of hours late coming home, he punched her.

"So anyway, when my mother came back across the border— she had a two-week pass, that's why she came back—he was waiting. He was mad, jealous. He started to yell at her, accuse her of things, right in front of people, right at the border. So he starts beating her, punching her hard. That is when the border people shot him. I've heard some people say that they just threw his body in the river, but I don't know if that's true. I was at school when it happened."

"SHE JUST HAD AN UNHAPPY LIFE"

Manuel's voice gets a faraway tone to it, remembering. He shakes his head.

"My mother, she just had an unhappy life," he says, "because there was more that happened to her than that. Maybe you could

Manuel's life has been filled with hardships, ranging from his parents' early deaths to his own trouble with the law.

say that it happened to me, because it made me sad. You see, even though my mother escaped being killed by my father, she ended up dying because of another jealous man. She was so young, too, only twenty-nine.

"Her new boyfriend—I guess he was just like my father had been. It makes me feel very bad inside that she was treated that way. But her new boyfriend was jealous and angry, too. I found this out one day when one of the holy fathers at the school sent for me, and I went to his office.

"He said, 'Manuel, I have something bad to tell you. Your mother is dead. She was killed in a bad car crash, but someone did it on purpose. Her boyfriend was jealous and drunk and forced her into a car and drove the car—BOOM!—into another car. They both were killed, and that was how he wanted it.' So my mother died, she just died.

"I guess her boyfriend told her, 'I'll die, but you will, too.' It seems such a sad way to die, I thought. That's why I don't want to be that way with ladies. Sometimes you get mad—everyone gets mad—but you can't go around hitting and pushing. I know that. It's better to walk around, go outside or something. If you do something, you might always regret it; the lady could get hurt. Or killed, like my mother."

Manuel says that he felt sorrow when he was told the news. The bad news was compounded, however, because he was informed that because his mother had been paying his tuition, he was no longer able to remain at the school. Life, he says, was going to change.

ON HIS OWN

He was sixteen, and unsure about how to proceed, he says. He had a sister, but he wasn't sure how to get in touch with her; it had been many years since he had seen her. And without either a mother or father, his prospects of finding a home seemed dim.

"The school told me that I probably have some aunts and uncles, but they didn't know where," he says. "They said, 'Manuel, here is one hundred pesos. You go now; you find them on your own. We can't help you.' So I left the school and started to look.

"I walked and walked, through villages, through the cities, asking people if they'd heard of anyone with my same last name or the name of my mother. Eventually, I found someone who wasn't related to me but who knew my uncle. He lived two hours away, and I walked to see him."

Manuel says that the meeting between him and his uncle was emotional.

"He didn't know me, but I told him about my family, and he agreed I was his nephew," says Manuel. "All the family names were the same. And he cried; I cried, too. We were so glad to know each other. He said I could stay there for a while, until I knew what I was going to do.

"I hoped he would let me go back to the school," Manuel admits with a smile. "That was really all I knew. I had friends there; I knew what I was supposed to do. But my uncle took me aside and said, 'Manuel, you are crazy! You cannot go back to the school; I cannot afford to send you there!'

"He told me that [that] part of my life was all over. It was time to make money, to do things like a man. So that is what I did. I did odd jobs, worked a little. It was not a time I remember with happiness, I suppose."

Was it pleasant living with a family again? Manuel considers the question, frowning.

"I don't know. He was a drinker, lots of beer. Did I love him? I don't know. He was my family; all I had. So I guess I did. I really don't have any feelings about him. I can't say."

FROM KIDNEY STONES TO HEAVY DRINKING

Manuel says that his days of working were frequently interrupted by health problems. He learned in 1968, at the age of seventeen, that he had kidney stones and that to remove them, he would need an operation.

"It hurt me so much," he says. "I would try to urinate, but it would be hard. And my body hurt all the time. Sometimes I would have a fever, get the chills.

"I did not get help, though. Not for fifteen years! It was expensive to have operations in Mexico, and no one would pay for me. My uncle tried to talk me out of it because he had fears. See, it is hard to explain . . . but then, in Mexico, there were many people who thought that by having an operation, you would get much sicker and die. It was a bad idea, especially for a young person. So no one would sign for me, take responsibility for my operation."

With medical help not an option, he sought relief from the pain in other ways.

"I started being a drinker," he says. "I drank a lot, and that made me feel better. And sometimes, I'd go to the city, go to places and get drugs—shots to take the pain away. I guess it was morphine or something. I don't know, but it helped. So that and drinking got me through the pain so I could do things sometimes."

"A LONG TIME CROSSING"

It was during this time, Manuel says, that he began toying with the idea of leaving Mexico and heading north.

"I had no mother, no father," he says. "I know I had my uncle, but he didn't care that much for me. It seemed like a good adventure to cross into the United States, nothing sad at all. I had nobody to cry for me, so it was easy to leave."

Emotionally easy, perhaps, but Manuel admits with embarrassment that physically leaving Mexico became a three-year occupation for him.

"It took me between seventy-five and one hundred times to do it," he says, with more than a trace of defensiveness in his voice. "I was a long time crossing. I was in no hurry; there was no rush for me. It was not like some who have friends or family in the United States. Those people are in a rush to join their husbands or wives. I took my time."

But how could he have failed so often? Why did he get caught by border patrols time and time again?

"I was drinking a lot still," he says. "I guess I didn't care too much whether I got across or not. I'd try crossing in California, then I'd try in Arizona—Nogales. Then Port Isabel, Texas, and New Mexico. Sometimes I'd get stopped by the border patrols as I was crossing; other times I'd make it across then get caught later.

"Other people would tell me, 'Manuel, you aren't doing it right. You don't get it. You got to get cleaned up, shave or something. You don't look like you belong.' See, I was all dirty, and I didn't care. I didn't hire no coyote—those people steal your money. I didn't want somebody cheating me. Besides, I didn't even have enough money to think about buying help. The money I made came from working a couple of hours someplace, just enough for beer and cigarettes. No money to be saved that way!"

"I LOVED THE LIBERTY!"

Success came, says Manuel, by riding freight trains between Mexico and the United States.

"Those trains come across the border all the time," he says. "Most of the time there are guards who check in those boxcars, take a look to make sure people like me aren't in there. But I got lucky. I hopped a train coming over [to] Las Cruces, in New Mexico. And once I got across, I thought, this is the life for me!"

Manuel smiles as he recalls how excited he was, traveling by train around the western United States.

"It was a free life," he says. "I loved the liberty! I said to myself,

After seventy-five to one hundred failed attempts, Manuel finally crossed the border into the United States. "I was a long time crossing," he admits, "I was in no hurry."

'Manuel, you were crazy before, sitting back in Mexico, doing nothing. This is good for me. Good for me!'

"There was always something new to see. I changed trains whenever I felt like it. I went to Oregon—saw lots of forests and mountains. I'd see California and Arizona. When I was tired, I'd get off a train and camp out under a bridge somewhere, take a bath in the river.

"I didn't need money," he says, smiling slyly. "I had hands and fingers. I could go into a town and take what I wanted. I would steal, yes, but only the things I needed. I'd take cigarettes, food, shoes. I'd take gloves, tortillas. These things I'd put in my back-pack and keep. I know it was not right, but I needed those things. I had nothing else.

"Besides," he adds, "I was not greedy. My needs were few. I'd get a radio for a dollar at a Salvation Army store and steal some batteries. I'd have music on my train! But I would never steal a television or something like that. I was not a thief like that."

Manuel insists that he noticed a big difference between being a poor man in Mexico and in the United States.

"You can't ask people for things here," he says. "You'd scare them. In Mexico, you knock on the door: 'Hey, lady, can I have some food?' She says okay and gives you a little, and you go on your way. Or maybe she says no, and you go away. People help, or they say no. That's all. But here they get afraid, call the police. I didn't want anything like that to happen."

SETTLING DOWN

During those days, Manuel says, he became a loner.

"I stayed to myself. I talked to nobody, because back then I didn't know any English at all. I didn't know who to trust, so I trusted no-body. And when my kidney stones made me sick, I drank my beer. It was a nice life for a time—a good life for me, for a little while.

"Some people say that they could do that forever, just ride around. They say it is like being on a vacation, one that lasts your whole life—a vacation you don't pay for. But I got tired of it. I'd get cold sometimes on the train at night. I had no blankets, just a little thin backpack. Nothing in there to keep me warm, and when I didn't have food either, I got so cold! I cried one time because I was so uncomfortable.

"I said to myself, 'Manuel, this is not right. You have to pay attention to what you are doing. This is sometimes fun, but not something to do forever. So I went to Omaha for a while, and then I heard that Chicago was a good place—lots of Mexicans there. I decided to settle down and earn some money."

In Chicago he was able to get part-time work doing construction on a low-income housing project for Mexican immigrants. He worked for his room and board and was satisfied with the arrangement. However, he says, his old health problems were becoming more and more acute, and he knew that his drinking was getting out of control.

"I knew I needed to get the operation, but I still didn't have any money," he says. "And then I met someone—a priest. He was a very nice man, very nice. He told me that I should go back to Mexico and get the help I needed. There was a hospital there that might let me have my operation for free, since they took care of poor people like me. The priest even gave me money, five hundred dollars, to fly back there! So back I went. I was going to get my operation and then return to the United States as a healthy man."

TO THE THIRD FLOOR

The journey to Mexico for the operation, however, took a strange twist after he went to the hospital. Instead of recognizing his symptoms as those of a person suffering from kidney stones, the staff at the hospital thought that his need for mental treatment was even more acute.

"There was a third floor in this hospital," says Manuel. "And all they did was treat crazy people. They told me, 'Manuel, you're crazy. You don't need to worry about kidney stones, you need to get better inside your head. The drinking and everything is making you crazy!'

"I was so surprised. I was drinking a lot, so I thought maybe the beer *had* made me crazy. They told me the best thing was for me to be there on the third floor for a while, and they would try to fix me up. After a while, they started with the shocks, the electric shocks. They put straps on my head and held my hands and legs down. And then I'd get shocks—sometimes three times each day."

Manuel says now that he is convinced that this hospital was taking advantage of its poor clients. Those people who could not pay were often used as test subjects and guinea pigs for experimental procedures, especially in the hospital's psychiatric ward.

"I didn't like it at all," he says firmly. "But I didn't know what to do. I thought, maybe I am crazy like they say. So after a while, they let me go home to my uncle's house and come in for the shocks during the day. And later they gave me a prescription for some blue pills, for me to take. They said they would help me feel better after I was not coming to the hospital anymore."

"I REALLY GOT CONFUSED"

The doctors told Manuel that he needed to be careful in taking the pills, since they should never be used with alcohol. Manuel says that he tried to follow their orders but admits he slipped up after a time.

"I had gone with my friend to a [soccer] match, and he said, 'Hey Manuel, how about a beer?' I thought one beer would be okay, so I did, but then I really got confused. It wasn't from the beer; I think it was the pills. That scared my friend, too. He didn't know what to think. He said I was staring at him like I didn't know him and that I got lost and couldn't find my way out of the stadium.

"I started drinking again, though, and I wasn't taking the pills anymore. They were so expensive, and I didn't have insurance

When not at work, Manuel clears branches and helps maintain his landlord's yard. Although his health has improved, Manuel blames the electric shock treatments he received in Mexico for making him disoriented and confused.

45

that would pay. There were lots of times when I got mixed up, and I think it was from the shock treatments I had. Besides, the pills didn't help my kidney stones and I still had pain from those!

"One time, my uncle noticed that I was having these—I don't know—spells, I guess you'd say, where I would get mixed up. He'd say to me, 'Hey, Manuel, what were you doing last night? We saw you sleeping in your closet!' I guess I got confused and couldn't remember how to find my own bed to sleep in."

Manuel says that he has never gotten over those times of confusion.

"Some people think I am just stupid," he says, "but I don't think that is right. I think it is just the shock treatments that weren't good for me. They should have helped me—that's what those doctors told me. They said they would make it so I wasn't crazy.

"I'm not stupid, and I don't think I was ever crazy," he says. "I forget things real easy, though. Like at work, if someone sends me to do a job, like painting or something, I have trouble remembering the address. If I'm not in an area I know, I have trouble. I lose my way real easy. One time I get to the house to do some painting, and the lady isn't home. I was late, because I'd had trouble finding the house. So I think maybe she got mad and left, since I am late.

"I sit and wait and wait on her steps, hoping she would come home. But she still didn't. So I walk to a pay phone and call the number on the paper I had, and the lady answers! She says, 'Manuel, where are you? I have been waiting two hours, and you don't come!' I say, 'Really? I knock and knock on the door, but you don't answer!' She says, 'Really? How many times?' And I say, 'Over and over, but you don't answer the door.'

"Then she tells me the address, and I see I had it mixed up all along. I looked at it before, but now it looks different. The numbers say 85, but I saw 58, I think. I feel bad when that happens, because I don't want the people to think I am stupid or that I am lazy and don't want to work."

"I DON'T WANT PEOPLE MAD AT ME"

Manuel says that the problem affects the way he listens to instructions, too, and that can be a real problem in his work as a handyman.

"Sometimes a customer says I should clean the windows outside. The guy tells me before he leaves. He says, 'Manuel, make sure you clean them just the way I am telling you.' And I don't understand. So when I do the job, I maybe clean the windows from the inside instead of the outside. And then he comes home, and he's mad because he says I didn't listen.

"One time a man told me, 'Manuel, see those flowers? There are too many weeds in there. You have to clean the flower bed out, get rid of all those weeds.' He asks me if I can do that. I say 'Sure, I can.' But then I do it all wrong. I cut all the flowers, and he gets so mad. He says, 'Manuel, I will not pay you; I don't want you here anymore. You are stupid, and you don't speak English.'"

He says that it makes him feel sad and frustrated when people get angry with him.

"I broke three windows at a lady's house," he remembers, shaking his head sadly. "She had told me to clean the windows, but she said to be careful with three of them, since they were hard to open. She told me, 'Manuel, do it this way, and don't be rough with them.'

"But I forgot, and they broke when I pulled them open. So the agency I work for—the people who send me out on these handyman jobs, they had to pay seventy-five dollars for those windows. I had to pay that back, too. I asked my boss why we had to pay, and she said, 'Because you don't listen, Manuel. You need to learn to pay attention when people tell you things.'

"She's right," says Manuel. "I try hard, but I have to try even harder. I don't want people mad at me. Now I write things down, even directions on how to do a job. I look at it again and again so I don't forget and do things wrong. I think I'm getting better at it. But those shock treatments—that is why I have the problem, I think."

"Never Give Up on God"

The kidney stone problem—which is why he originally went home to Mexico in the first place—was solved eventually, he says, and more quickly than the chronic confusion that was probably produced by the electric shock treatments.

"I was still in Mexico, and the pain was getting bad, worse and worse," he says. "I went to this other hospital, walked right in the office at the front. I told them I had no money but that I was really hurting, all around my side, my back. This one lady, she says, 'Manuel, you go outside and wait; I'll come out and talk to you in a little while.' So I did.

Manuel listens to his landlord's instructions about the yard work. Chronic confusion has caused Manuel to make many mistakes in his handyman tasks. "I try hard, but I have to try even harder. I don't want people mad at me," he explains.

"After about half an hour she comes out and tells me that I am very lucky. She says, 'Manuel, do you know that Jesus loves you?' I said, 'Yeah, I know he does.' She said, 'You should never give up on God.' And I said, 'I know that, lady, I know that.' And she said, 'Manuel, I am a doctor, and I will do the operation for free so you do not hurt anymore.'"

He was so happy, he says, that he could hardly believe she was telling the truth. However, in just two days he was admitted to the hospital where she was a surgeon, and he got his kidney stone operation.

"That was one of the nicest things anybody ever did for me," he says. "I didn't do anything to deserve it; it just was something that happened. She didn't want my money or anything. She was just a good person, and she told me to take care of myself, so that I could live a long life.

"I try to do that," he says.

After recovering from his operation, Manuel crossed the border again and found his way back to Chicago.

"It was a good place to live for a while," he says. "I had friends there who were in a gang. I wasn't in the gang. I just would sit around with them sometimes, drinking beer, listening to the radio, maybe playing soccer sometimes. There were some dangerous people around there, but I was safe when I was with those guys. I knew I wouldn't be getting beat up.

"The only time I had trouble was [when] a man came after me in the street with a knife. I had a knife, too. He was drunk and wanted to kill me over nothing. He was shouting and yelling, and people heard and called the police. I could hear them coming; you could hear the sirens getting closer and closer. I saw a bottle lying there in the street, and I threw it at him. I was mad that he came after me for no reason, I think.

"Anyway, I got away from that man before the police came. See, I didn't want to be there when they arrived, even though I didn't do anything wrong. I had no papers. What if they sent me back to Mexico? So I left, hid out for a while."

Manuel says that he left Chicago because the Immigration and Naturalization Service began doing sweeps in the area in which he was living.

"There was some bill passed in Washington," he says, "and the government decided to limit the number of immigrants. So every day, the INS cars would come and the agents would look for Mexicans. A priest that I knew there said, 'Manuel, if I was you, I'd get out of this city now. I hear there are good jobs north of here, in Minneapolis.' So that's what I did—I came here."

"I DID IT WRONG, BUT I'M WORKING ON IT"

Manuel says that he has made efforts to become legal, but that things haven't always worked out.

"In Chicago I called an immigration lawyer. He told me to come in on the first of the month. That was on a Sunday, and no one was there. I waited, but, really, no one came, because the government is closed on Sundays. He got mad at me later and told me I made a mistake. He said, 'Manuel, I never told you to come on Sunday.' But he did.

"So anyway, I was supposed to go in again. I could get a document that was a special paper that immigrants who had been here for five years or more could use. I didn't get that done, though. I didn't go to the appointment with that lawyer.

"I got another appointment when I came to Minneapolis," he continues. "I got temporary papers, but not [final,] legal ones. They told me I had to wait until my papers were all processed, and then I would come in for another appointment. But then I got in trouble and went to jail for breaking that girl's glasses. So I missed that appointment."

Manuel admits that the trouble he has had in getting his papers has been of his own doing.

"I have made mistakes, I know that," he says. "I did it wrong, but I'm working on it. With my record, I have to wait about five more years to start over with the papers. That makes it hard to get work, too. I like it that I work here at this place. It is an agency that a group of churches run together. I do work for old people or for people who are disabled, can't move around. The people at the agency tell me when to go out on different jobs.

"I have a goal: to get permanent papers. I don't want to worry about being sent back to Mexico. I don't know what I'd do. I want to make my life nice, and the only way to do that is to work hard and save my money."

No Drinking, No Smoking

Manuel says that when he got out of jail, he knew he had to do something about his drinking. He began going to Alcoholics Anonymous meetings at a community center in the city.

"I was going every day for a while," he says. "It was good for me to do that. There are people there who have stopped drinking, who haven't had any drinks for ten or twelve years, and they *still* come to the meetings! It was hard for me to believe that they still needed to come for support after all that time. I didn't want anybody to be in control of my body like that, so I stopped drinking pretty fast. And when I did, I stopped going to those meetings. It just seemed easy for me.

"And one more thing happened because of those meetings. I would notice that so many of the people there smoke—all the time, lots of cigarettes. I noticed that, and I said to them sometimes, 'You gave up drinking, but you start smoking! Why is that? You are addicted to something else now!'

"But people get angry when I tried to point that out to them. I wasn't mad at them, so I don't know why they were mad at me. I was just showing them what they were doing. I'd say, 'My friend, don't get mad at me. It's not my life; I was just telling you.' But they still got mad, and still smoked and smoked.

"But not me, I stopped that, too. I was smoking four packs a day sometimes. And you do smoke more when you want a drink—I know that."

Manuel smiles. "You know how you should quit? This is what I did: I would put tobacco in my coffee and drink it. It would make me sick, make me throw up. See, the tobacco is poison. After a while, your body has enough, and you can't even think of tobacco anymore. So you stop. It's a hard way, but it works."

"TOO SCARY"

Manuel lives a pretty solitary life today. He works alone, checking in daily with the agency that sends him on handyman assignments.

"I call to see if they need me to clean, or paint, or something like that," he says. "I live upstairs in a lady's house. She is letting me stay there free while I help her get her house ready to sell. I come and go as I please.

"I never have gotten married. I almost did once, in Mexico, when I was very young. We were engaged, but after a while, she said, 'Manuel, I don't want to get married; and besides, you're ugly.' I told her I didn't mind not getting married. And I told her she was ugly too," he says with a smile.

"But now, I just am by myself. I don't complain, though. I like it that way. I get nervous around people. Like yesterday. I was forty-five; it was my birthday. And the ladies here at the agency, they are very nice. They had a cake for me, a little party. I left real fast, though. It was too scary for me."

He has conversations with other Mexicans he knows, people he sees here and there. However, those encounters frequently leave him irritated, he says.

"There is so much bragging, so much playing games. One guy I talked to yesterday was telling me what a failure I am, because I don't have a car. He drives a nice one, and he laughs at me, with my bicycle. He has lots of nice clothes, too.

"He says, 'Manuel, look at you, working and riding your bicycle. I get nine dollars an hour, and I live pretty good.' I told him, 'My friend, I don't care. I am putting all my money in the bank. I am saving my money, so even though I don't make a lot, I put it in the bank for later."

Some of Manuel's acquaintances ridicule him for riding a bicycle, but Manuel says he prefers to save his money and live modestly. "I don't want to be on the streets when I'm an old man," he says.

Manuel says that in addition to the bragging he gets tired of listening to the complaints of other immigrants who are not doing well.

"They say, 'Look at me, Manuel. I was an architect back in Mexico, and here I am washing toilets or picking fruit. Americans don't like us, they give us no opportunities.'

"But I know that is wrong," he says. "They are not really what they say: they were not architects or engineers or anything like that back in Mexico. If they were, why would they have left? They just need people to blame. They want an excuse for their own mistakes, I think."

Asked if he confronts them in those conversations, Manuel shakes his head.

"I try to get by, be okay with everybody," he says. "If they want to think they are rich making nine dollars an hour or poor because they are Mexican, they can do that. I just keep working, even if it is for a lot less money. I don't want to be on the streets when I'm an old man. That's what I know for sure."

Carolina

"WE ARE NOT TRYING TO BE RICH
OR TO HURT ANYONE. AMERICANS
MUST UNDERSTAND THAT MOST
MEXICAN PEOPLE—MOST
CENTRAL AMERICAN PEOPLE—
WHO COME HERE ILLEGALLY, WE
HAVE NO OTHER WAY TO LIVE."

"I would not have thought, when I was a little child, that I would be one of those Mexicans who would be sneaking across the border, hoping to find a better life in the United States," says the woman with the long black hair. "My life was good; my family was well off. We were not the sort of people that would have to scurry across the border to make money. We owned lots of land, and my father made a great deal of money.

"But look now," she says, pointing around her small apartment. "Here is where I live; here is where we have come. My family is here, living a secret, pretending to be legal immigrants from Mexico, when we are nothing of the sort. I am happy to have visitors, happy to tell my story. But I want to be sure again: are we very certain that my name, the names of my husband and my family, will not get into the hands of the INS?"

Also, her husband, Ramon, she says, is quiet and shy and would prefer not to be interviewed. Carolina, Ramon, and their family have been in the United States for three years. Carolina is only forty-three years old, with five children and, she says proudly, five grandchildren! Their home is small but tidy and neatly decorated. Colorful posters and family pictures hang on the living room walls.

"This is my youngest daughter, Rosalia," she says, picking up a framed photograph from an end table. "She is the only one of my children who still lives at home. She is in seventh grade now, a very smart girl. The other children are older, off on their own. All of them are here, living in the United States. And like us, all of them are waiting to become legal. Until then, we hide."

A PLAN GONE WRONG

Carolina spent her early years on a large ranch owned by her father. She says that they were wealthy, with lots of cattle and horses.

"We were not like most people in Mexico," she admits. "There is so much poverty, so many people who do without even basic things. But we were always comfortable; there was always more than enough to eat. We were a large family, too—seven girls and four boys. I was the middle child. I was not looked after like a baby but old enough to do plenty of chores and babysitting myself!

"My brothers and my sisters and I went to Catholic school in Mexico, run by French priests and nuns. I loved school; I loved math and grammar especially. History and geography were not my favorite subjects, but I managed to do well enough. In my mind, I planned that I would concentrate in high school on mathematics. I wanted to be an accountant, to learn to make budgets and organized plans for business. That sounded like something I would really enjoy."

Carolina says that it was her father's untimely death that resulted in a major change in her family's plans.

"The ranch was taken over by my uncles," she says. "They were not as capable as my father had been, and they misused the money. They spent too much, made too little. Pretty soon there was hardly any money at all for us to live on, and my mother announced that we had to leave the school. It was a luxury now; it was far more important for us to get jobs and earn some money for the family."

A WIFE AND A MOTHER

Carolina got a job in a funeral home in town. Although it was not exactly the job she'd dreamed about back in school, she was glad to be able to help out with expenses.

"I was overqualified, I guess you would say now," she says. "I answered the telephones, took messages, handled the bills. I was not an accountant, and it was hard to imagine working in this

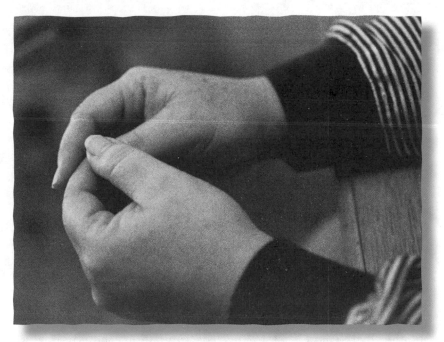

Before her father's death, Carolina says her family was wealthy and lived comfortably in Mexico. "My life was good; my family was well off. We were not the sort of people that would have to scurry across the border to make money."

place for the rest of my life. I felt sorry for myself a little; I was only a teenager and missed my friends back in the school. I missed that life."

It was not long until she met Ramon, a handsome young man just five years older than she. The two fell in love and married.

"It was exciting to be off on our own," she remembers, "but there was a feeling that without my paycheck, my mother would be having a harder time raising the younger children. So Ramon and I took two of the youngest ones to ease the burden. And the years went by, with us raising them, as well as children of our own.

"Ramon did not have as much schooling as I had, but he knew a great deal about construction. He was what you would call here a 'jack of all trades.' He knew welding, carpentry, plumbing. He was a handyman. So he was able to move from job to job, doing whatever needed to be done in the construction of houses and other buildings."

Hard times hit Carolina and Ramon several years ago. Ramon became ill, having pain in his back and his joints. Working on construction sites became difficult for him.

"The doctors said that he has a disease that is making his bones dry and brittle," she explains. "He got some therapy for it in Mexico, but it was not helping as much as he had hoped it would. He went to the Mexican social security office to see if he could get some retirement benefits. We hoped that if he could get some money from those benefits and if he could cut down to working part-time, that would help.

"But they wouldn't allow it. Ramon had no choice but to continue working, and that was so painful for him. I took in laundry to make a little extra money for food, but that was not much help. Ramon and I were worried, and we weren't sure what we should do."

Carolina says that there was something else that was becoming more and more an issue: Ramon's age.

"It is not like here," she says. "In Mexico, it is almost impossible for a middle-aged man to find work. You have no trouble being hired if you are seventeen or eighteen. Up to twenty-four, maybe. But after that? There is a lot of age discrimination. They think you cannot do the job well after that.

"It's different if you already have the job; they won't fire you if you are already hired. But you see, Ramon was a handyman. He worked at one site, then moved to another when the work was done. He was not a permanent employee with one company. So as he got to be thirty, and thirty-five, he was not the one being hired. It became harder and harder for us to get by.

"MAYBE FOR A YEAR OR TWO"

Carolina says it was not a difficult decision for them to come to the United States, primarily because they were only going to do it temporarily.

"We knew people who had come to the United States," she says. "We had heard about the economy, how it was easier to make a lot of money here than in Mexico. Some of our relatives had come up—my younger brother, as well as several of Ramon's relatives.

"But it was too much to consider moving away permanently! We had friends and family in Mexico. Our life was there, even though it was a difficult one. We would go to the United States, we decided, but only for a while, maybe for a year or two. We would make money and then come home and live better."

The family would not all cross the border at once; rather, they would go gradually, with Ramon and their oldest daughter going first.

"It was not terribly difficult for them," says Carolina. "They crossed the first time; the two of them got separated. My daughter, who was twenty at the time, was detained and was told to go back to Mexico, while Ramon got through easily. They'd made a plan, though: if either of them were to get caught and sent back to Mexico, they were to go to the house of some relatives we had in Tijuana. So when my daughter was caught, Ramon went back to Mexico and found her, and they crossed the next day, I think it was. It was not a problem.

"Ramon was gone for two years, and I missed him terribly! He stayed in Los Angeles first, since he had a sister there. Someone told him about Chicago, and how there were so many more job opportunities there, so he went east. And when Ramon had stayed there for a while, he got in contact with another relative, who recommended he come north. It is very difficult to travel alone in a new country, for one must depend on other people's information. It was so lucky that Ramon had the advice of his relatives and friends!"

LEAVING MEXICO AT LAST

Carolina says that after two years Ramon returned, anxious to take more of his family across the border.

"It was always in stages, and I think that's why we did not have difficulty, as some Mexican people do," she explains. "I have heard so many stories about people being robbed and beaten, lost in a strange city, or separated from their young children. But our family just went gradually. We did not go in a large group—no calling attention to ourselves in that way. A few at a time, that was the key for us.

"Ramon took our son then later came back for me and one of our grandchildren. Each time someone new came over, there would be family all settled, waiting for him. It was much easier crossing when you knew that at the end of your journey there would be a sister or an aunt and uncle who were waiting with a meal and a bed for you!"

Carolina says that when she came across the border, she was very nervous. Her husband had paid coyotes to make fake papers for them in case anyone questioned them.

"The border guards asked why we were crossing, and we told them we were going shopping for the day in the United States," she remembers. "Our papers looked fine to them, but my heart was beating so fast I almost couldn't hear their words!"

TROUBLE FROM A COYOTE

"The only one in our family who had a bad experience was one of our sons. My husband and I had already crossed, and we had become separated from him. He was arrested and sent back. He found another coyote to help him, but this man was a cheat. He sent my son a different way, and he was lost in the [Mexican] desert. My son eventually got in touch with us in the United States (we had given him a number where one of Ramon's relatives lived), and he talked to the coyote we had used.

"Things worked out that time, although we had to spend more money," she recalls. "Let me see . . . Ramon and I paid our coyote $800 just for crossing the border into California. That covered the fake papers, too. And another $550 for the plane ride out of San Diego. And our coyote offered to get our son out and all the way north to where we were for an extra $800. That was a great deal of money, but we knew it was a better deal than any other of the coyotes would offer. And besides, we had learned to trust this man.

"He was true to his word, too," she says happily. "My son joined us here very soon after he talked to us. It was so nice, being together again. My daughter was already here, but with problems, unfortunately. She had a husband who was drinking and hurting her, going out with other women. She was glad to see us, for she had been so lonely and sad, always by herself. It was good that we were all able to come here, to the same city, and be supportive for her when she was so much in need."

Carolina says that coming to the United States meant more to her youngest daughter than simply seeing relatives and giving support to family members. Rosalia had done a great deal of research into her new home, her mother says, but not all of it was accurate.

"She had seen too much television," says Carolina with a laugh. "She had seen shows about all the mountains and lakes, the beautiful scenery in the United States. But of course, those things weren't there the moment we crossed the border. Rosalia did not understand; she was only ten years old at the time. She kept asking, 'Mama, where are the mountains?' She was so confused!

Rosalia (pictured), Carolina's youngest daughter, was only ten years old when she made the journey to the United States; Rosalia was disappointed when she crossed the border and did not see the beautiful scenery portrayed on the American television shows she had watched.

"She was not sad about leaving, no. It was not like here, where friends are the most important thing. In Mexico family is more important, playing with brothers and sisters. My children were together a lot, and Rosalia was a girl who loved her family, even though her siblings were older than she."

GETTING WORK

There was little time for Carolina and Ramon to worry about what they had left behind in Mexico. The most important thing was for them to find work to support their family.

"For me, I did the same as I had done back in Mexico," she says. "I took in laundry. But at the end of one month I was amazed. Back in Mexico I would receive about 50 cents for my work. Here, my first month's salary was $170! Ramon and I just laughed and laughed. All thoughts of staying in this city for just a month or two and returning to Mexico vanished. I thought, why would I go home? How foolish I would be!

"For Ramon it was not as easy. Because he was illegal, he did not have the papers necessary to do the kind of work he was used to. Here in the United States, plumbers and welders need licenses and certificates. But Ramon could not apply for those things through the state, as a citizen of this country could.

"It is too bad," she continued, "because men who have the skills Ramon has, who have these licenses, can earn a great deal of money—between eighteen and thirty-three dollars an hour. That would be unheard of back in Mexico. But Ramon does the jobs for only $7—if he can find an employer who will hire him. For a while he did what he did in Mexico, work as a handyman, going from job to job. Now he and my older son work in a lumberyard. It is heavy work, and Ramon's bones still bother him. But he rarely complains."

As her family has become more comfortable in their new home, Carolina has taken a factory position in addition to her laundry work at home. She works the late shift at a plant that makes the metal logos that are placed on new cars.

"I took the job because I can work while my husband is home with Rosalia," she explains. "I would never want to leave Rosalia at home alone, for she is much too young. But I can bring in more money than simply doing laundry, and Ramon can be at home with her. And the money I get is very good—$6.15 an hour."

No Options

Carolina knows that she and the rest of her family are quite lucky to have come safely to the United States and are fortunate to have jobs. Part of her is very grateful, she says, but she also realizes that there are many Americans who resent Mexican immigrants being here.

"People are people," she says matter-of-factly. "We are all some-times quick to judge others without knowing them. I don't think we mean to be rude or narrow-minded when we judge people, but we do it out of ignorance. My children have noticed that there is not much in American schools taught about Mexico or politics there. Maybe that is why some people are resentful of our being here.

"Some American says, 'Oh, I cannot find a job. I cannot pay for my house, my food.' So maybe he looks around and sees me work-ing in the factory, making money. So then he says, 'See, if it weren't for those Mexicans, those immigrants sneaking here into my country, taking all the jobs, I'd be better off. I could have *her* job.'

"But that is not really how it is," she says. "I know there are plenty of jobs. I cannot look at it that I am taking an American's job and that I am hurting an American. If someone wanted that job, why didn't he take it before I came here? Why don't they fire me and hire an American for that job? I don't know the answer, but I know that there are jobs like that for all."

Carolina understands that there are laws about coming into this country illegally, as she did, and she admits that sometimes she feels ashamed, but only for a moment.

"You see," she explains, "Ramon and me, our coming here with our children and grandchildren—this was not just for fun, for adventure. We are not trying to be rich or to hurt anyone. Americans must understand that most Mexican people—most Central American people—who come here illegally, we have no other way to live.

"In Mexico there are few jobs; there is little money to be made. And for our children, it is not all the time that breakfast is on the table. That is so! School is not someplace where the little ones automatically go each day. For many families it is a decision, a choice. When we see there is no money for breakfasts, when we are poor, we say, 'We have to decide. Do we send the children to school, or do they go to work out in the fields or the factories? That is true. Even for very young children there are hard days at work.

"That is bad, and Ramon and I know that. We do not want to live like that, worrying about our children, our grandchildren. Even when we are working hard, to have such little money to show for it is discouraging for us."

Carolina shrugs. "Yes, it is awful to feel that we are illegal, that we are breaking laws just by being here. But I cannot apologize for trying to help my family. There was no other way for Ramon and I to help our family. We have no options; that's why we came. It is to save ourselves. To sink or swim, Americans say—that is right."

BEING LIKABLE

Carolina says that while she cannot change the way some Americans feel about Mexicans, she can try to make sure that people know that *she* is a good person.

"I work right alongside many different people at the factory," she says. "There are whites, Southeast Asians, black people. I am easygoing, likable, so I have no troubles with my fellow workers. I try to give them the same respect I'd like them to give me. I give a smile, try to be friendly always. No problems. See, once people know you, wherever you come from, they can see whether you are a good person.

"Really, the only person that has really discriminated against me is my supervisor at work, a white woman. For some reason, she does not like me, and I do not know why. I am sure it is not because I am not a good worker, because I know that I am. I never complain; I work hard.

"In fact," she continues, "when I first began this job, the first supervisor was very nice. She was so kind. She would show me a new job on the [assembly] line and watch me for a while. She'd say, 'Good, good. You are a quick learner. Good for you!' But this new lady came a couple of years ago, and things have been different almost from the beginning."

Carolina pauses, as if reconsidering what she has said. She looks troubled, as though she has perhaps spoken too much. She shakes her head at the interpreter and speaks rapidly to him.

BURRA!

"I do not mean I do not love my job," she insists. "I do. I don't want anyone to think I am ungrateful. I will do any job they want me to do. I should not have complained. It is only that I wanted to explain about the lady who is my supervisor."

What is it exactly that she doesn't like about her supervisor? Carolina looks embarrassed.

"She yells at me always," she says. "She gives me the hardest jobs, the worst ones. Like maybe the parts of the assembly line that are the slowest, the most difficult. Like those jobs that involve using pliers—those are slow. And then she stands behind me and screams."

Carolina does an impression of a stern-faced woman, hands on hips, yelling, "*Rapido, rapido!*"

She shrugs again. "I do not like that, especially when I am going as fast as I can. To move more quickly, I might do the job wrong, and that would anger her even more. Some of the others on the line say it is because I am Latina—a Mexican woman—and maybe that is so.

"Again, don't think of me complaining, but I will say this. I don't

At times, Carolina reminisces about her life in Mexico. "I miss my friendships back in Mexico. . . . But most of all, I miss being a homemaker," she admits.

like being taken out of the line and given the job of cleaning the bathrooms, scrubbing the toilets and floors. Only me! None of the other workers are selected to do that or are pulled aside. The Anglos, the African Americans, the Asians—none of them are taken out.

"But no, she keeps it up. She calls me bad names, too. I think that is what angers me the most. She calls me slow, stupid. And sometimes the worst—*burra*," she says, rolling the r's with exaggerated disgust. "That is donkey, stupid ass. I got mad that time, stuck up for myself. I told her not to call me that and that I am not stupid or slow. She got even madder, though, and told me that I had to leave my job."

Carolina smiles. "Three days later, though, her supervisors found out what she had done and knew she was wrong, so I came back to work. I have my old job back. I was so glad. So I just keep working now, grateful to have a job. I will not complain again, for this job buys food for our family! I would be a fool to complain about it, right?"

Sometimes, she says, when she is home alone in the afternoon, before Rosalia comes home from school, she thinks about her home in Mexico with some sadness.

"It is not as though my life is completely here now," she says. "There are certainly things I miss. One of them is the weather! This ice and snow during the winter . . . and the winter goes on so long! It makes me tired and makes me long for the warm sun back home. I admit, in the winter I try not to go out very much, just back and forth to work.

"I miss my friendships back in Mexico, too. It was so nice to have people to talk to—other women whose children were my children's age. And we could sympathize with one another about how difficult and silly they sometimes were!

"But most of all, I miss being a homemaker," she says sadly. "I loved being a wife and mother all the time. I do love it here in the United States, and I am happy. But I find that it is hard to keep our home clean, to do all my cooking, preparing food the way my family likes it. I must be gone so much, working, and doing the laundry for money. I get so busy with outside things that I feel that I neglect sometimes my most important duties, do you understand?

"I used to make my own tortillas, spend more time cooking," she continued. "Not from cans, or jars. That part was better in Mexico. We had little, but I was always at home, always here for my children. I love being a homemaker. I am amazed sometimes how many women find it a burden they would like to be rid of!"

No Difference in Children

Asked if she finds it more difficult to raise children in the United States than back in Mexico, Carolina shakes her head.

"I think raising children is difficult wherever people live. There are so many things to remember, too many opportunities to go wrong. I have heard other Mexican women complain that the United States is too lenient with their children, too easy. But that is foolish, I think. Who is raising the children? Not the country, not the government! It is the parents.

"There are undisciplined children here, just as there are undisciplined children in Mexico. That is not a reflection on the government, I think, but the parents. Maybe those parents do not take an active role in teaching them right from wrong. Maybe those little children spend too much time unsupervised, right?

"I don't agree with some from my country when they say children need more spankings, more beatings. We don't need to brutalize them for mistakes. But parents need to make sure the children understand when they've made mistakes. I have tried to do that with my children, but sometimes I wonder! There are always times when parents feel as though what they're doing is not

Trying to stay out of view, Carolina stands on the porch of her apartment while her daughter Rosalia relaxes on its steps. "I think raising children is difficult wherever people live," Carolina says, discounting the notion that it is more difficult to rear children in the United States.

enough. And then we wonder, what should we have done, or what did we do wrong?"

To make matters worse, there is what Carolina sees as a credibility problem in the United States that she says does not exist in the same way back in Mexico.

"It seems that when the police or the government gets involved in a problem that has to do with a family," she says, "they believe the first one they talk to. Now if I were to do that as a parent, it would be crazy! So often it is not the one doing the tattling who is the real victim but the one who keeps silent. That business of who to believe, I think, is a real problem here and can hurt people in the family who are doing nothing wrong!"

"IT WAS SUCH A STUPID STORY"

One such instance, Carolina says, is something which she says hurts her so deeply, it is often difficult to talk about.

"Our second-oldest daughter did something very wrong not long ago," she says quietly. "She abandoned her husband and children and went off who knows where. No one knew where she had gone, and she did not call. We were very worried.

"She was gone for a month and a half. Our son-in-law dropped off the little children with us, for he could not care for them. He had to work during the day. So the babies lived with us, you could say, for all that time."

Carolina says that after a month and a half, they received a telephone call from the city police. She says that the police were on their way over to talk with Carolina and Ramon, along with agents from child protection services.

"What had happened," she says quietly, "is that she knew that she had done wrong. She had gone off with another man and had left her husband and her babies. So instead of coming back in shame, admitting she had made a mistake, she took the offensive.

"She accused me and Ramon—her own mother and father—of mistreating her children while she was gone. She claimed that she had known we were being mean for some time, and that was why she left."

Carolina shakes her head and looks disgusted.

"It was such a stupid story; it did not make any sense at all. So completely a lie! But the police and child protection people believed her story right away, at least for a little while. So for a short

66

time, people who did not know us, who did not know how we love those children, they believed Ramon and I were capable of such things! They said we mistreated them in many ways—hurting them, not giving them proper food and clothing.

"My daughter—we do not speak her name in this house any longer—she was ashamed of what she had done, like I said. Rather than own up to her own mistakes, she made up lies that hurt me and hurt Ramon. Ramon and I had to go to court and be asked all kinds of questions."

"WHO WOULD BELIEVE US?"

Carolina admits that she was frightened of the court appearance and that she lost a great deal of sleep worrying about it.

"I wasn't nervous about anything I had done," she says. "It was only that by going to a court, going to the government, I worried that we would be found out as illegals. And we did not speak any English at all, so who would believe us?

"But they provided us with an interpreter in the court, and the people asked us all sorts of questions. Nothing about our illegal status even came up—I guess because it was not a criminal matter but a family one.

"In the end, of course, it was all sorted out. The judge, the police, child protection—they understood we would never have been abusive like she said. Like I said before, my daughter made up such a stupid lie, so easy to disprove. She told the police that we would only dress the children in raggedy clothing, and that we barely fed them and they were starved.

"But even the police said that was not true, for when they had come to our house, they could see the children were well fed and happy and that my house was very clean, very tidy. Their clothes were clean and neat. The social workers said that, too."

Carolina looks sad for a moment then composes herself.

"There is no longer a relationship between us and our daughter. Her husband and the children are always welcome here. In fact, they are coming by later for dinner. The oldest one, Juan Pablo—John Paul—is the apple of his grandpa's eye! He is so happy, so full of fun. And so good with games. I think he will be a mathematician someday or a computer genius!

"But Ramon has suffered a great hurt. It caused him such pain, that his own flesh and blood would accuse him of hurting his

Carolina says she feels somewhat disheartened that her youngest daughter, Rosalia (pictured), is becoming so Americanized. Carolina hopes that her children will retain their Mexican roots, even though they are so far from their homeland.

grandchildren. She used us, and that can never be forgiven in this house. She lives with them—I suppose she no longer carries on with that other man—but she does not come here ever."

In Carolina's view her family is still a Mexican family rather than an American one. That fact makes her happy.

"It is not that I find fault with Americans," she says. "I do not.

But we are a long way from being Americans, in everything we do. Language, for instance, is something we have not changed. Ramon knows a little [English], but not much. He gets out much more than I do because of his job and the lumberyard. And Rosalia has learned English from school. But we all speak Spanish here, and it is difficult to ever imagine a time when that will change.

"Now Rosalia," she says, with a wry grin, "*she* is very good at using her English in certain situations! When she is on the phone, for instance, and doesn't want us eavesdropping on her private, important conversations. And when she has friends over here at the house, they speak in English, I think, because they do not want me to know what they are planning! Actually, I think all teenagers would do that if they could speak a different language from their parents, if they thought it would keep us old people confused!

"I am proud that Rosalia has learned English so well, but I do think that she is getting into some bad speaking habits here. I don't think this is a word that means anything in English—*nyuh, nnyuh*! She says it all the time on the telephone with her friends. I ask her, 'Rosalia, what does that silly word mean, that you say all the time? It sounds like you are chewing gum when you talk!' But she just laughs. Teenagers!"

WE EAT MOSTLY MEXICAN

Another aspect of their lives that hasn't changed much is the food they eat. Carolina says that she cooks Mexican meals almost every day for her family.

"It is cheaper than American food, I think," she says. "Potatoes, rice, beans, vegetables, a little meat—that is inexpensive. Plus we are all used to it. I feel badly that I do not make my own tortillas any longer, for as I said before, there is not the time there once was for me to cook all day. But there are many conveniences one can buy in the grocery store, and the food is good. So five days a week we eat Mexican. On the weekends, sometimes, we go out for hamburgers or pizza. And even I admit that it is fun for a change!"

Carolina says that she wants her children to always be aware of their Mexican roots but that sometimes it is difficult, especially for her youngest daughter.

"Rosalia wants to be liked; she wants to fit in. And that usually means being like American girls—at least in many ways," she says. "I understand that. I try to, anyway. But when we talk about things, about memories of Mexico, and the people we knew there, she is not interested.

"Rosalia has *plans*. She likes to study hard, for she is very smart. And she wants to go into computers someday. She is even planning on taking a summer school course on advanced computers. I think of summer school as a punishment, for students who do not do their work during the year to catch up. But for Rosalia, no. She wants to learn, do more, be with her friends. When we talk about going back to Mexico someday to visit, she gets very unhappy. She would not come along, she says."

"It's a Good Sign"

Carolina says that life for her family of illegal immigrants has been scary sometimes but that she is optimistic that things will turn out well for them.

"We got a letter recently from the INS, saying that they have accepted Ramon. He will be legal sometime, they say. We are just not certain when that will be done. But eventually. It's a good sign—that things will be okay for our family. But really, until we have those papers, very officially signed and dated, we are still illegal. We must still fear being caught and sent back.

"I do know that it is not always the end of the world if you are caught by the INS, for it happened to Ramon three years ago! The INS started randomly stopping Latinos around the city, checking their papers to see if they were fake. And they would go to places immigrants would likely work—factories, fields, loading docks—where there is heavy work to be done.

"Ramon was seized, but they gave him a break! They told him they would not send him back, but he had to get to work right away on applying for legal status. And yes, he took their advice, and got busy! They have been giving him extensions for this, so that he can get it done, for the government moves very slowly. He has a temporary work pass, and when that expires, he is supposed to get another. And sometimes it comes, and sometimes it doesn't; we don't know why.

"For that reason," she says, "it is always in the back of my mind, that our luck might run out. This is such a big country, with so many people . . . I hope they remember us! I hope those papers do come. Then I can stop being nervous, worrying all the time."

Jose and Maria

"IF . . . WE DO NOT GET OUR
PAPERS, THEN WE WILL MOVE
OUT OF THIS COUNTRY, LOOKING
FOR ANOTHER REFUGE. . . . BUT
NO, WE WILL NEVER GO BACK. I
FEEL AS THOUGH WE ARE
LEFTOVERS FROM DEATH,
SURVIVORS. AND THAT LIFE IS
OVER NOW FOR US."

The door swings open and a very short smiling woman opens her hands in welcome. Her hair is very long and streaked with gray. Her voice is high pitched and loud and becomes even more so when she notices that one of the visitors is an old friend named Patty.

"Ahh!" she squeals happily. "Patricia, Patricia!" She gives Patricia a hug and beams with pleasure at three-year-old Ian standing close to his mother's leg and at baby Abe, whom she has not yet met.

"Maria and Jose and their family are good friends of ours," explains Patty to the other visitors. "I met her when she first came here and helped her find housing for her family. Our families have become close friends in the last six years."

Maria and Patty begin to chat in Spanish, while Maria's husband Jose walks in and says a shy hello. He invites everyone to sit down around the kitchen table.

A HOUSE IN THE PROJECTS

Jose is a handsome man, with a thatch of gray hair. He smiles, but the smile does not quite reach his eyes. He is a man, it seems, who is carrying deep sadness.

The family has lived in this project in St. Paul, he explains, for the past four years. The living room is a rather cold space, with walls of whitewashed bricks and linoleum floors. A television and VCR take up one end of the small room. The furniture is both shabby and comfortable, with stains from years of spills. What can you expect, Jose says, with grandchildren around all the time?

The kitchen is obviously the room where the family spends most of its time. There are the good smells of cooking carrots and beans, and Maria is humming as she slices potatoes, too. On the wall is a large color picture of President Bill Clinton, with the word *Si* above it. Another wall holds a crucifix and a calendar showing a scene from Central America.

NOT EASY TO UNDERSTAND

The family has come to the United States from El Salvador, a country in Central America. It is difficult to understand how urgent their need was to leave El Salvador, says Maria, because so few people in the United States are familiar with El Salvador's situation.

"It is a country torn apart by a war," she says, as Jose nods in agreement. "There is no peace there. There hasn't been for many years. It is the government fighting against the guerrillas, the army of the poor people."

Jose explains that in El Salvador most of the people are very, very poor. He defines himself as a campesino, a peasant who owns no land and who makes up the lowest class in El Salvador.

"We were better than some," he insists. "Many campesinos have no homes at all. They live in ditches along the roads or in boxes made of cardboard. The children of peasants almost never go to school; instead, they work in the fields alongside their parents.

"There is no hope for people like us in El Salvador," he says. "And the government is corrupt, a government made up only of the wealthy and the military, who want to keep power. Anyone who rises up, who challenges those people, is brutally tortured and killed by the government death squads. That is why many of the poor have formed their own armies, fighting guerrilla-style. They wage war against the death squads, against the government—but it is very dangerous work."

Joining the guerrillas *is* dangerous, as Maria learned firsthand. She lost eighteen members of her family—brothers, cousins, and sisters—in battles and raids by the government forces. And in 1986 their oldest son was killed.

LIVING IN A CONFLICT ZONE

"He had joined the guerrillas," says Maria quietly. "He wanted to help his people. But we lived in such a dangerous place, directly in a zone of conflict, and he was killed in 1986. Ramon was only twenty-three when he died."

Another son, only fourteen at the time, was killed by government forces while he was visiting a nearby Catholic mission.

"He was so young," says Jose in a tender voice. "He was killed as a bomb fell from the sky, and when it exploded, he was hit by shrapnel. He was standing next to a tree, not hurting anybody. Just standing by the tree."

Maria remembers that more than anything she wanted to visit the place where he died.

"Friends said to me, 'No, no Maria, don't go to that place,' but I had to see where he died," says Maria, choking on the words. "I

Jose (right) and his family immigrated to the United States from the war-torn country of El Salvador. "There is no peace there. . . . It is the government fighting against the guerrillas, the army of the poor people," his wife Maria explains.

needed to see it before I could believe it. I cried and cried afterwards, but it was something I needed to do. It was such a waste—so many young people, so many lost."

"WE WOULD ALL LEAVE IN THE NIGHT"

As all of the peasants in that zone of conflict soon learned, it was not only the soldiers who were endangered by the fighting. Almost monthly there were raids by the death squads, looking in villages for guerrillas or even guerrilla sympathizers.

"There would usually be warnings," Maria explains, "where we would hear that troops were approaching. We would all leave in the night, leave our houses, our animals, whatever we had. We could not take anything, just the clothes we were wearing. There would be long lines of us heading for the mountains, heading for safety. We hoped that the darkness would make us less visible to the death squads.

"And while we were there, the squads would sweep through the villages and destroy everything, burn everything in their path. They wanted to teach us a lesson, show us how heartless and cruel they were."

Maria remembers with sadness how many of the mothers of the village would leave behind very young babies when a warning came about the approach of death squads.

"They knew a baby's cry could endanger the entire village," she says. "That was probably the most common way soldiers would find people in the mountains, in fact. I suppose it made sense in a way. Maybe they hoped that the child would survive, while at the same time they were unwilling to risk the whole family or village being discovered and tortured and killed."

"I TOLD JOSE, 'I'M GOING NOW'"

Maria says that she knew she could never sacrifice a child of hers that way, however. She remembers vividly going up into the mountains during a raid, when her youngest child, Julian, was just an infant.

"I couldn't leave him," she states flatly. "I would never forgive myself if something were to happen to him and I wasn't there. I would rather die myself, you see. I just figured that if I was going to die, I would die alongside my children.

"So one time—Julian was still a tiny baby—we were hiding

very high in the mountains. He started to fuss, and everyone was worried. I told Jose, 'I'm going now.' So I ran away from the rest of the group and threw myself down a drop-off, like a small cliff by a creek. I lay on top of my baby, trying to muffle his cries. But he still could be heard, and I knew I had to do something!

"I took a rag from my pocket and stuffed it into little Julian's mouth. It was so big [that] it cut both sides of his mouth. I felt so horrible for hurting him, for making him bleed. I picked him up again and ran over to the creek and grabbed a handful of little pebbles. I threw them into the water, trying to distract him from crying. We spent the whole next day there, the two of us. I just held him and patted him, and finally he fell asleep! I still remember little Julian, how I felt so guilty for stuffing that rag in his mouth. But then I think, what was the alternative? It was better than being shot, I know."

Stepping over the Dead

The raids usually lasted for four or five days and sometimes more than a week. When the peasants felt the danger was over, they would make the long walk back to their village. It was always the same, says Maria.

"We would walk slowly, for we were very tired and hungry. We had not eaten for days, and the children were so weak [that] even some of the older ones needed to be carried.

"We were thirsty, too, and we eagerly drank the water from the creek. It did not matter if there were dead bodies upstream, in or near the water. We did not worry about the water being contaminated. We only thought of our thirst and how bad we felt.

"And as we got closer to our village, we could see the smoke rising, we knew our houses were gone. We stepped over the bodies of horses, of the animals. We stepped over the bodies of people, too, people who had not gotten away in time. And everywhere there were the dogs feasting on the dead. I can never forget those times. They went on for more than ten years for us. Imagine—ten years of our lives hiding, scurrying to get away. Yes, we were survivors, but what a long, difficult time that was!"

It Was Time to Go

Although Jose and Maria often talked about leaving El Salvador for somewhere safe, it seemed an impossible dream.

"Besides the two sons who died, we had four more children," says Jose. "And there were checkpoints all over El Salvador, places where troops would be patrolling. Surely a journey like that would be very dangerous for our family! Believe it or not, we were actually safer in guerrilla territory, since they did their best to protect us. Outside of this zone we would be beyond their protection; we'd be on our own.

"But as the years went by, we knew we had no future in El Salvador. It was death, bombs, guns shooting all the time. And we knew we had to act soon, because the war was only intensifying."

Jose says that the family moved from their dwelling in the conflict zone to a village near a city. He got part-time work there as a construction worker, earning money for their journey.

"We used that time to plan, too," says Maria. "We plotted and thought all the time, Jose and me. We decided that at first the two of us would go alone. We used all our money, plus some we borrowed from friends and family. Our four children we left with relatives so they would be looked after while we were gone. It was so hard to leave them, but we told ourselves that it was for just a little while."

"GOD WAS WITH US"

There were several stages to their journey. Jose and Maria had to travel from El Salvador to Guatemala and into Mexico. From Mexico they would try to sneak across the border into the United States.

"We traveled in stages, gradually," explains Jose. "We came to Guatemala easily enough. We spent a night or two in cheap hotels because we did not want to spend our money on anything fancy. After we were lucky enough to escape being shot at in El Salvador—truly, we did worry about that quite a bit—we had no fears in Guatemala.

"From our country to Guatemala was no problem. Borders are not guarded as they are in the United States and in Mexico. The countries of Central America, like Guatemala and El Salvador, along with Costa Rica and Nicaragua, are called sister nations. They are under one constitution. We can travel back and forth easily between those countries. But Mexico—that was another story."

Jose says that he and Maria worried as much about being detained by Mexican border patrols as by U.S. immigration officers.

"The Mexican patrols are posted all along the border between

Maria describes how her family escaped from El Salvador as her friend looks on. Jose and Maria's journey to the United States took sixteen days. "The most exciting part was when the coyote helped us across the border from Mexico into California," Maria says.

Mexico and Guatemala," he says. "They are called the Mexican Rangers, and they can be very dangerous. They are soldiers, so they are very quick with guns—plus, we knew that they would be angry at us if they caught us. They would shoot us, detain us, send us back to El Salvador. Any of those things was frightening to us. Maria and I had no false documents. If we had been caught, we would have had nothing to show, no excuses."

Maria, listening with interest, nods her head excitedly.

"God was with us," she says, smiling. "He knew we were devout Christians, and he helped us, pushed us along. We made the journey safely in—what was it?—sixteen days. The most exciting part was when the coyote helped us across the border from Mexico into California.

"We came with two men and four women, plus a twelve-year-old boy. The men the coyote put in the trunk of his car, and the women were stacked on the floor of the back seat with the boy, lying under blankets. It was so hot, so stuffy with all those bodies, but we were not stopped."

Once Jose and Maria were settled in the United States, they worked hard and saved their earnings, hoping to raise enough money to bring their children across the border.

Jose and Maria established temporary living quarters in Los Angeles, living as cheaply as possible. They both found work, intending to save money to pay coyotes to bring their children to the United States.

"We saved four thousand dollars in eight months. That was how cheaply we lived," says Maria. "We rented the living room of an apartment, not even the whole apartment! We lived in an area of the city called Little Tijuana because of all the Mexicans that lived there. The money we were saving was going to be sent back to El Salvador. We intended to send for our daughter, Marta, and our youngest son, Julian, to come first. The other two boys, Carlos and William, would come afterwards.

FINDING WORK

"We found that it was difficult to find jobs in Los Angeles. Without papers proving we had social security numbers, we could not get good-paying jobs. Jose was able to find two days of work each week in construction and made a lot by El Salvadoran standards—$110 each day. However, for the wage scale of the United States, and compared to the wages of other construction workers with papers, it was not a lot. It was difficult to save money, for everything cost so much!"

Maria says that she found a job pushing an ice cream cart along the beach everyday.

"I would go to the ice cream factory, get the cart and ice cream for the day, pay for it, and then take it out to the beach. I pushed it all day, often very late into the night. Sometimes I was still selling at midnight if the weather was hot. By the time I got the cart back and cleaned out, it was two or three o'clock in the morning. Everyday, more ice cream for the people at the beach. How much did I make? It varied. Sometimes I'd make eighty dollars, sometimes only forty dollars. All I remember was that I was so tired on some of those days, and so busy, that I didn't have time to eat at all!"

Jose adds that another source of income for them was turning in aluminum cans for recycling.

"We would get up very early in the morning and look for beer cans, pop cans, anything we could find," he says. "We'd collect them in big plastic bags and turn them in for money. It wasn't much, but every dollar we made was important, for it meant that we were that much closer to having our children join us in the United States."

"Eight months after we arrived we brought Julian and Marta over," says Maria. "They had no problems; they were very fortunate. But soon afterwards Jose and I became nervous about where we were living. There was so much crime and so much pressure for the young people—gangs and things.

"I had heard about Minnesota from a friend we had met. She

had an aunt who lived here and said there were many more jobs in the north. She said it was a nice place, pretty, clean cities. We didn't know too much more except that there weren't as many gang problems here and it was close to the Canadian border. We saw that on the map!"

They decided that Maria would take the two children, and Jose would stay behind in Los Angeles, working and saving money to bring the other two children up from El Salvador.

"We came on the bus," she remembers. "It was New Year's Eve when we left L.A. It took us three days on the bus to get here. Some friends came along, and we had been assured that my friend's aunt would allow us to stay in her home for a while until we got settled. She met us at the bus, in fact, and drove us to the west side of the city, where she lived.

"Oh, it was cold!" laughs Maria. "I had *never* believed one could be so cold! You could make clouds with your breath, and our lips and fingers turned blue! But we were happy to be here in St. Paul and glad that we had a friend to stay with.

"But our happiness did not last long, unfortunately. The aunt changed her mind about having visitors stay with her. I think it was nothing we did particularly; it's just that she wasn't used to noise. She and her husband lived a quiet life alone in that house. But six of us, with the children, camped out on the floor—that was too much for her! We were paying rent and everything. We had given her money in advance. But she told us, no. We had to make other arrangements."

FINDING HELP

Maria and her children left the house at dawn the following morning, hoping to find a place to live.

"We wandered around the west side, where many of the immigrants live," she says. "I had heard about a Guatemalan man who worked nearby, who ran a church organization to help people get settled. It was something I'd heard through the grapevine, you know? He was supposed to be someone who cared. So the children and I went to his office, and we waited a long time, but he didn't come. It was a disappointment, but we figured we would find another way.

"So we went back on the streets, and there we met two other men. One was from El Salvador, the other from Guatemala. They were happy to see me, especially the man from my country. He asked me many questions about how long I'd been away and how the situation was there. I tried to answer him as well as I could and told him how things were for us right now, about how we were looking for a place to settle.

"Well, he was very nice. They both were. The man from El Salvador said, 'You are my countrywoman; you shouldn't still be suffering now that you have come here to the United States! You should come home with us, back across the river to Minneapolis. You and your children can stay with us for a time until you make a plan."

Delighted, Maria and her children went to Minneapolis with the men and stayed for a little more than a week. By that time, she says, she knew that she had to find work and a place for them to live as a family.

"We first went back to the home where we had first stayed and got our belongings," she says. "Then we went back to the office of the man who was supposed to help people. And it was a good thing, for he helped us almost right away!

"They told us about transitional housing we could get while we were waiting for a real home. In fact, they started the paperwork right away. By that night we were settled in a motel in downtown St. Paul, right by the convention center. For our meals all we had to do was to walk across the street to the Dorothy Day Center; it is a drop in center run by the Catholic Church. They help people in need. In fact, that is where I met Patricia!"

Patricia smiles. "I remember the first time I saw you and your children. You looked so cold. The children had no hats, no gloves. I don't think any of you were prepared for how cold it gets here, and it was the coldest time of the winter. At the Dorothy Day Center we were able to assist you with that, too. People donate lots of warm clothing just for that purpose."

Maria grins, remembering. "I had sandals on, I am sure. I was so glad for those socks and shoes you gave me! And we could stay in that transitional housing for three weeks, and you assigned us a social worker, who helped us find a real home."

WAITING FOR WILLIAM

"We rented the bottom part of a duplex. We contacted Jose, and he made arrangements to join us. He had sent money to El Salvador for twelve-year-old William to make the journey. His older brother, Juan Carlos, had joined the guerrillas and wasn't ready to leave yet. So little William would join another family and make the trip north without his brother."

However, Maria says, their plans were not successful at first.

"William was detained at the Mexican border," she says sadly. "But the coyote didn't wait for him or help him at all. He just took off—ran with the money he had not yet earned.

"Poor William; he was so scared. We heard later that he cried and cried. The family that he was traveling with got through, so he was all alone. You see, that is when your heart breaks, to hear about such things that your children face when you are not there to help them. It made me feel sad for William, that he had to be there alone, feeling the way he did. But he remained brave inside, and he did the best he could.

"What really frightened me was that when he was finally sent back to El Salvador by the Mexican immigration authorities, he was in such poor condition," she says. "The relatives with whom

Shortly after Maria and her children arrived in St. Paul, they met Patricia (left), who worked at the Catholic center where Maria was able to obtain winter clothing for her family. "I remember the first time I saw you and your children. You looked so cold," Patricia recalls.

he was staying told us that he was both dehydrated and malnourished when he arrived. I do not know if it was because the immigration people did not feed him or if his condition was due to the stress and nervousness he suffered."

"SIX TOGETHER, FINALLY!"

What Maria *did* know, unfortunately, was that they had invested a sizable amount of money in bringing William to the United States, and instead both he and Juan Carlos were still in El Salvador. Thousands of dollars spent, and they were no better off than before.

"We just got busy again, working, working. We heard from Juan Carlos that he was ready to come north, so he would accompany William whenever we could send the money. So when we accumulated four thousand dollars, we sent for them and waited. We prayed a lot, too.

"In the meantime, we moved from that duplex to this place in the projects. It is bigger, with more room for the six of us. And this is where the boys joined us. And we were six together, finally!"

Maria says that the reunion with William and Juan Carlos was one of the happiest times of her life.

"We had a great party, a celebration," she crows. "We had so much to be thankful for, so many blessings that day! We had music; there was a priest there who played accordion. No, there was no dancing. You see, we are very devout Catholic people, so there are many things we don't do. We had no tequila, no cigarettes, nothing like that. It does not mean we are unhappy—my goodness! We enjoy life so much, but we like a home that is good for children, where what we do is good for them.

"There were so many people who came to welcome Juan Carlos and William, so many friends we had made. Patricia and her new husband, Doug, were there and many people from the church we went to. There were so many, and I decorated the house so pretty, with signs, flowers, lots of balloons."

Maria scurries into another room and brings out a blue photo album.

"See," she says. "This is Jose, looking so proud. And here is the priest I was telling you about. What a grand party. It was like a thanksgiving, a way to praise God for all the blessings we had: coming to this country, finding work for Jose, and having all of us who survived that terrible war, all together in one place."

"Being Honest Was Best"

Asked if his illegal status worries him, Jose says he is of two minds.

"Yes and no," he says with a half smile. "First of all, it was hard to be nervous and worried after we arrived here, after going through all the hardships in El Salvador. We were so lucky. It did not seem possible that we would be sent back after all that.

"And another thing, we presented ourselves to INS when at last all our children had arrived. Being honest was best, we decided. We told them our story and asked for political asylum. That is granted by the United States sometimes when people have arrived here from a nation at war, a place where their lives were in danger [because of their political beliefs].

"Was I nervous about going to the INS? Oh, yes. I was nervous all right. But to my surprise, I did not need to be. They were very understanding, and they knew about the situation in El Salvador, how bad things were there. They issued us work permits so that we could earn our own way while we were waiting to see if we

Jose and Maria applied for asylum through the INS once all of their children were safely in the United States. "Being honest was best, we decided. We told them our story and asked for political asylum," Jose explains.

would be granted asylum officially. Our permits were temporary—good for six months at a time. Each time they expired, we would go to INS and renew them. After a year of that we were given permits good for one year."

Jose says that the INS has offered them no guarantees, but reports that the authorities say they are optimistic.

"They think things will work out well for us," he says. "Since then we wait for the document that will give us official status as having political asylum. In the meantime, we are working hard, Maria and I. We both work at the potato factory. She has been there six years, doing different jobs. She works on the line, sorting the potatoes, and in the cleaning service, making sure the dining room and other facilities are neat. I work on the loading dock, loading the crates of potatoes into trucks. I've been there five years now."

CHILDREN GROWING UP

As Jose finishes his story, Maria takes Patricia's son, Ian, into the kitchen.

"You want to help me make lunch?" she asks him. "How about we make some good food for everyone, and you can be the helper?"

The three-year-old nods, not understanding the Spanish language. But clear about the friendly intent, he walks shyly, his hand in hers. Soon Maria is telling him about the good food she will serve with her tortillas: beans, rice, carrots, and potatoes. As the visitors follow the good smells into the kitchen, Ian stands proudly next to Maria at the stove, holding the lid of a pan.

"It is so nice to have little ones around," she says. "My daughter Marta has two children of her own now, Rosita and Kimberly. It is such fun having them visit, giving them hugs and kisses! They grow up so fast, just like my four have.

"It is hard for me to imagine Marta having children of her own. She was just a little girl when we arrived here. I remember the thing she was most excited about when we moved to this place was having her own room. Back in El Salvador our house had been so little [that] we all shared a room, Jose and I and the children. So when she was given her own room here, she was delighted. She had room for her things, room to hang her pictures on the wall, and even room for a mirror!

"Juan Carlos has a business, roofing houses. He has worked very hard learning English and getting his business going. He is twenty-four now, a man. And William is following close behind; he is eighteen. He had trouble for a while in school—smoking pot, hanging around with boys who were not a good influence on him. He wasn't doing well, but since then he has been placed in an alternative school. They teach everyday skills like balancing a checkbook, using the newspaper, things like that. He is doing very well, and we are proud of him. William is training to be an apprentice to a painter, so he will earn good money later on. He is a good boy. We have always known that."

Her youngest, Julian, is now fourteen, and a student at the local high school. It is Julian, she says, who has been the most eager of her children to learn in school.

"He gets many compliments from his teachers," Maria boasts. "They say, 'Julian is one of the best students we have ever had here.' He is a good artist, and he has a quick ear for learning languages. Besides speaking Spanish and English, he is learning French in school. And he says he is not satisfied with that; he wants to learn Chinese next!

"I know he can do it. Here in the projects where we live, there are some Vietnamese and Hmong children, and he has learned many of their words already. I like that Julian is a good student, for that would not be an option for him back in El Salvador. He is hoping to graduate from high school. And who knows? Maybe he'll go on to college! Imagine!"

No Complaints

Are there things about El Salvador that Jose and Maria miss, even though they are happy in the United States? Jose speaks first.

"There really aren't too many things about El Salvador [that] I think about in good ways, to be honest. There was so much violence, so much hardship. It was not a good place for our family to stay. I do miss my mother; she is still there. But it is painful to think about her, too. Most likely I will never see her again, for if we are granted political asylum, we will never be allowed back. That's the rule: we cannot set foot on that soil again, even for a short visit."

"I miss lots of things," says Maria. "I miss my family, I miss preparing foods in the traditional ways, the way I used to. I miss the little river where we used to go and swim and fish. El Salvador is a hot climate, tropical. So I have to say that I miss the sun six months of the year!

"But I have no complaints. Yes, there are differences, but in what is important, the United States is far better for us. As I said, back in El Salvador we would not be able to give our children education that we can give them here. That is an important thing. In the United States things are better. People here *want* children to learn, want there to be nice classrooms and books for all. Bright rooms and nice teachers who are sympathetic and who listen to the children who have trouble sometimes in learning things."

Maria says she has heard other immigrants talk about the prejudice they have encountered here but that she and Jose cannot complain.

"We have been told that because we are fairer-skinned than some other immigrants, we perhaps haven't felt the same kind of prejudice. Maybe that is true. And of course, there are racist people, people who think we are taking advantage of the people of this country by coming here. Some act as though we do not belong because we speak another language. But racists are everywhere, in every country.

"I think the United States does very well, considering how many different people, different cultures, exist here. There are problems, but how could there not be? This country takes on such huge responsibilities!"

IMPORTANT GOALS

Maria and Jose agree that the most important thing they can do with their lives is to keep their family close and continue to stress those values that they have always cherished.

"We do not go out too much," Jose says. "We don't go to the beach or to the parks very often. We do things together here at home. We spend time with our children, talking to them, playing games. On Sundays, especially, we set aside that time, to make sure we think about our blessings. We say the rosary together, even though the older boys sometimes are not too excited about it."

Maria says she enjoys doing pottery when she has a day off from work. She dashes upstairs and brings down a small cardboard box containing six pots and vases of various shapes and sizes, wrapped in newspaper.

Jose and Maria are haunted by their memories of El Salvador. "Some are easy to talk about, others are not," Maria comments. "I still remember how it sounded when the bullets were flying, zinging over our heads."

"I work with this white clay," she says. "I taught myself, too. I don't have a pottery wheel or anything like that. I just use a spoon and my own two hands. Sometimes I paint them; other times I leave them white. I sell them at craft shows sometimes, and that always makes me proud when someone buys something I have made."

She says that there is one goal she made for herself several years ago that she admits she hasn't done too well achieving.

"I promised myself that I would learn to speak English," she says ruefully. "But I haven't done that. For a while, there was a student from a nearby college who offered to come here once a week and help us learn, but I was such a failure! I think with Jose and me, we are older and our minds are too closed for learning English. I can hear a word, practice it all morning, and by the end of the day, I've forgotten it.

"Maybe some of that is because of the headaches I have, I don't know. I wake up every morning at about four o'clock with my head pounding. I don't know if I am sick or [if] the headaches are caused by bad dreams. Maybe it is stress from our life back in El Salvador. I am not sure."

LOOKING FORWARD

Jose and Maria say that while their new life in the United States is happy, they are both plagued by vivid memories of the fighting and violence they endured in El Salvador.

"There are too many things, too many memories," Maria says. "Some are easy to talk about, others are not. I still remember how it sounded when the bullets were flying, zinging over our heads. Everywhere there was the smell of the gunpowder burning. I sometimes look at my children growing up and say, 'Is this the little boy I ran with, who I comforted when he was so afraid of the noise?'

"One of the worst things was that my children actually got used to the danger. They were accustomed to death, to sights and smells of the dead. That is terrifying, that such things can become almost normal for children. How can they adapt to that kind of life? How can children in Bosnia or anywhere?

"And I look at Jose and remember him carrying the two older children, while I carried the two younger ones—one in front, one in back. I remember walking to the mountains when I was so pregnant. Oh, my back hurt, carrying little William! My legs hurt, too, and I was light-headed from not eating. And trying to get comfortable, lying down, with the rain falling."

What would they do if they were not granted asylum? What if they were sent back to El Salvador? Jose shakes his head emphatically.

"We will never go back," he says firmly. "El Salvador is our country, and we love it, but we will not repeat the history of that place again, not with ourselves, not with our children. If for some reason the immigration people are wrong and we do not get our papers, then we will move out of this country, looking for another refuge. Maybe Canada. But no, we will not go back. I feel as though we are leftovers from death, survivors. We have been spared. And that life is over now for us."

Epilogue

As *The Other America: Illegal Immigrants* goes to press, there have been some changes in the lives of the people whose stories it tells since their first interviews.

Manuel continues to see his probation officer regularly. He is still at his handyman job, although severe bouts with bronchitis have made work difficult. His doctors have told him that the change from warm summer weather to cold autumn is hard on his lungs and makes it difficult for him to breathe.

Carolina is at her same job at the factory and says not much is new in her household. Her oldest son recently came up from Mexico and is now living with Carolina. Her daughter Rosalia continues to do well in school, especially in history and computer class.

Jose and Maria are happy that their daughter has moved into a nearby apartment in the same projects in which they live. They enjoy seeing so much of their grandchildren, they say. Their oldest son, who has built up a successful roofing business, is now thinking of moving back to El Salvador. He says he still does not feel completely at home in the United States.

Alicia and her children are excited because her husband has recently returned to the United States after being captured and sent back to Mexico earlier this year. Her oldest son, Luis, had a great soccer season, scoring a number of important goals for his Division I team.

Ways You Can Get Involved

The following organizations can be contacted for more information about illegal immigrants in America:

American Friends Service Committee
1501 Cherry St.
Philadelphia, PA 19102

This organization believes in the dignity and worth of all people, and lobbies against what it feels are unfair immigration laws in the United States.

Federation for American Immigration Reform (FAIR)
1666 Connecticut Ave. NW
Washington, DC 20536

FAIR works to limit legal immigration, and to put a halt to illegal immigration.

Immigration and Naturalization Service
U.S. Department of Justice
425 I St. NW
Washington, DC 20536

The government agency charged with apprehending illegal immigrants.

National Center for Immigrants' Rights
1636 W. Eighth St., Suite 215
Los Angeles, CA 90017

An advocate for the legal rights of refugees and immigrants. This organization publishes a directory of agencies that will assist immigrants.

For Further Reading

Tricia Andryszewski, *Immigration: Newcomers and Their Impact on the United States*. Brookfield, CT: Millbrook Press, 1995. A very readable book explaining the impact of both legal and illegal immigrants in the United States. Good index.

Ted Conover, *Coyotes: A Journey Through the Secret World of America's Illegal Aliens*. New York: Vintage, 1987. Excellent resource for those readers interested in the relationship between the smugglers and the illegal immigrants who come from Mexico and Central America.

William Dudley, ed., *Immigration: Opposing Viewpoints*. San Diego: Greenhaven, 1990. Good selection of viewpoints on the question of open immigration and other topics relating to illegal immigration. Excellent bibliography.

Michael LeMay, *From Open Door to Dutch Door: An Analysis of U.S. Immigration Policy Since 1820*. New York: Praeger, 1987. Challenging reading, though extremely helpful in understanding how the American people's attitudes about immigrants have changed over the years.

Index

About the Author

Gail B. Stewart is the author of more than eighty books for children and young adults. She lives in Minneapolis, Minnesota, with her husband Carl and their sons Ted, Elliot, and Flynn. When she is not writing, she spends her time reading, walking, and watching her sons play soccer.

Although she has enjoyed working on each of her books, she says that *The Other America* series has been especially gratifying. "So many of my past books have involved extensive research," she says, "but most of it has been library work—journals, magazines, books. But for these books, the main research has been very human. Spending the day with a little girl who has AIDS, or having lunch in a soup kitchen with a homeless man—these kinds of things give you insight that a library alone just can't match."

Stewart hopes that readers of this series will experience some of the same insights—perhaps even being motivated to use some of the suggestions at the end of each book to become involved with someone of the Other America.

ABOUT THE PHOTOGRAPHER

Twenty-two-year-old Natasha Frost has been a photographer for the *Minnesota Daily*, the University of Minnesota's student newspaper, for three and a half years. She currently attends the University of Minnesota and is studying sociology and journalism.

When not working at the paper or going to school, Frost enjoys traveling. "It gives me a chance to meet different people and expand my knowledge about the world."